Why
Do We
Say It?

Why Do We Say It?

The Stories Behind
the Words, Expressions,
and Cliches We Use

CHARTWELL
BOOKS

Brimming with creative inspiration, how-to projects, and useful information to enrich your everyday life, Quarto Knows is a favorite destination for those pursuing their interests and passions. Visit our site and dig deeper with our books into your area of interest: Quarto Creates, Quarto Cooks, Quarto Homes, Quarto Lives, Quarto Drives, Quarto Explores, Quarto Gifts, or Quarto Kids.

This edition published in 2017 by Chartwell Books,
an imprint of The Quarto Group,
142 West 36th Street, 4th Floor, New York, NY 10018, USA
T (212) 779-4972 **F** (212) 779-6058 **www.QuartoKnows.com**

Chartwell Books titles are also available at discount for retail, wholesale, promotional, and bulk purchase. For details, contact the Special Sales Manager by email at specialsales@quarto.com or by mail at The Quarto Group, Attn: Special Sales Manager, 401 Second Avenue North, Suite 310, Minneapolis, MN 55401, USA.

10 9 8 7 6 5 4 3 2

ISBN: 978-0-7858-3570-7

Printed in the United States of America

SUSTAINABLE FORESTRY INITIATIVE

Certified Sourcing

www.sfiprogram.org
SFI-01681

Label applies to text stock

A-1. *Why do we use "A-1" to mean "the very best"?*

Because when the Marine insurance firms of London started the association later to become known as "Lloyds," they also started a register of ships and shipping in which the condition of the ships and their cargo was noted. The ships were graded by letter; the cargoes by number. "A" meant the ship itself was perfect; "1" that the cargo was likewise perfect.

Aback. *What is the reason we say that a person who is surprised is "taken aback"?*

It's a nautical term. When the sails of a square-rigged sailing ship are suddenly carried by the wind back against the mast—as sometimes happens in a strong gale—the ship is "taken aback" and stopped dead. So, too, a person halted abruptly by some new development is "taken aback."

Abacus. *Where did we get the name "abacus" for the counting device used by the Chinese and others?*

The device takes its name from the ancient Phoenician work *abak* meaning "dust"—because the mathematicians of that day used to cover tables with dust in order to draw their diagrams and figure their problems.

Abeyance. *What is the reason we say that something held up is "held in abeyance"?*

It's because "abeyance" literally means "hold your mouth open." The word comes from the French *bayer*, "to gape," and the allusion is to those who while waiting for something to happen stand with their mouths open.

Aboveboard. *Why is an honest person said to be "aboveboard"?*

Because card sharps and magicians place their hands under the "board," or table, to prepare their tricks and stack the deck. If they keep their hands above the board they can be presumed—not always accurately—to be proceeding without trickery.

Abracadabra. *Where did we get the magic word "abracadabra"?*

This cabalistic word, said to have been the name of the supreme diety of the Assyrians, was recommended by Q. Severus Sammonicus as a charm against ague and flux —if written on a piece of paper, hung around the neck, in this form:

<pre>
A B R A C A D A B R A
 A B R A C A D A B R
  A B R A C A D A B
   A B R A C A D A
    A B R A C A D
     A B R A C A
      A B R A C
       A B R A
        A B R
         A B
          A
</pre>

Abraham's Bosom. *Why are good people who have died supposed to rest in, or on, "Abraham's bosom"?*

Because it indicates the just deserts of the holy. It was the custom among the ancients for a person to allow a dear friend to recline on his bosom while eating. Only the dead who have gone to Heaven and there been welcomed by Abraham could hope to recline on his bosom.

Accost. *What is the reason a person who speaks to you without introduction is said to "accost" you?*

It's because he usually sidles up to you. The Latin word for "side" is *costa*—and "accost" literally means "at the side."

Achilles' Heel. *Why do we use the phrase "Achilles' heel" to refer to a man's vulnerable spot?*

Because Achilles' vulnerable spot was his heel. According to Greek mythology, Thetis, the mother of Achilles, dipped him into the River Styx in an attempt to render him invulnerable. Unfortunately, she held him by his heel as she did so. And thus his heel became his one 'vulnerable spot. Achilles died of a wound received from an arrow shot into his heel.

Acknowledge the Corn. *What is the reason "acknowledge the corn" means no acknowledgment at all?*

The story is told of a man who bought two flatboats, loaded one with corn and the other with potatoes, and sailed down the Mississippi River to make his fortune. Upon his arrival in New Orleans, the man went to a gambling house and there lost all his money—and the two boatloads of produce. On his return to the wharf, he found that the flatboat of corn had sunk. Later, when the person who held his notes for the produce demanded delivery, he said: "Stranger, I acknowledge the corn"—which was easy enough since the corn was at the bottom of the river—"but, by thunder, the potatoes you can't have."

Acre. *How did we get "acre" as a measure of land?*
The word "acre" originally meant a field—any field. But in the reign of Edward I of England an exact definition was set as the amount of land a team of oxen could plow in a day—40 poles long by 4 broad, or 4840 square yards.

Acrobat. *Where did the word "acrobat" come from?*
It is a Greek word which literally means "one who goes about on the tips of his toes and fingers." This is an accurate enough description of acrobatic dancers—but not of all acrobats.

Adam's Apple. *How did the voice box of the throat come to be called an "Adam's apple"?*
The term is an allusion to the story of the Garden of Eden. Supposedly, a piece of the forbidden fruit stuck in Adam's throat and created his "Adam's apple"—but women have them too.

Adam's Off Ox. *Why do we say something is as hard to recognize as "Adam's off ox"?*
Because Adam lived so long ago; because all oxen look pretty much alike; and because the "off" ox of a team of oxen is partially hidden from sight by the "near" ox.

12

Addled. *How did "addled" come to mean a person lacking in wit?*

"Addle" comes from the Anglo-Saxon word for "filth" —*adela*. An "addled" egg is a rotten egg—one which will not hatch and so perform its normal function. From an addled egg we get the whole idea of a person who is unable to perform his normal functions being "addled."

Adieu. *What is the origin of the word "adieu"?*

The word comes to us from the French *à Dieu*—a shortening of the phrase "I commend you to God."

Admiral. *Where did we get the word "admiral"?*

From the Arabians. The Arabian word *amir* means "ruler" or "commander" and *bahr* means "sea." An Arabian sea commander was called an *amir al bahr* or "ruler of the sea."

Adroit. *Why does "adroit" mean an adept and agile person?*

Because this word—which comes from the French *à droit*—means "to the right." The French presumed that only a right-handed person was skillful.

Against the Grain. *What is the reason we say that something we do not like "goes against the grain"?*

The allusion here is to the carpenter who tries to use his plane against the grain of a board. Instead of smoothing the board down, he roughs it up. So too, anything which "goes against our grain" roughs us up.

Agony Column. *Where did we get the name "agony column" for the personal notices in a newspaper?*

From the British. The London "Times" once devoted the second column of the first page to personal advertisements. These advertisements were so often full of cries of anguish from an aching heart that the column acquired the name "agony column."

Album. *What was an "album" originally?*

A table with a white top on which were kept the names of Roman officials and accounts of public proceedings which was prominently displayed in a public place. The word comes from the Latin *albus*, meaning "white." The British adopted the term during the Middle Ages and used it to signify a register or list of persons. From this, "album" acquired its present meaning.

Alcohol. *Did the word "alcohol" always mean "spirits"?*

No, "alcohol" originally meant "eye paint." The ancient Egyptians and later the Arabians used a fine black powder for tinting the eyelids. The Arabian name for this was *al koh'l*. From this any fine powder got the name—and finally the vinous spirits extracted by means of a fine charcoal filter came to be called "alcohol."

Alexander's Beard. *How did we come to "swear by Alexander's beard"?*

Alexander the Great of Macedon disliked hairy faces. He himself shaved and he ordered all his men to shave likewise—lest an enemy grab one by the beard and, holding his head, lop it off. So, to "swear by Alexander's beard" is to swear by nothing at all.

14

Alimony. *Why is a divorcée's pension called "alimony"?*

Because it's her bread and butter. The word comes from the Latin *alimonia* meaning "nourishment."

Alligator Pear. *What has the alligator got to do with the fruit known as the "alligator pear"?*

Not a thing. But when the people of one country take a word from another's language they often change its sound and spelling to make it agree with that of a word they already know. Thus the fruit called *ahuacatl* by the Aztecs came to be called *aguacate* in Spanish. But the French turned it into *avocat* or a "lawyer pear"—while the English made it "alligator pear."

Allspice. *Does the word "allspice" mean the seasoning is a combination of all spices?*

No. Allspice is a kind of pimento, dried and ground. It gets its name, however, from the fact that it tastes like a mixture of nutmeg, cloves, and cinnamon.

Alma Mater. *Why do we call the college which we attend our "alma mater"?*

Because this Latin phrase literally means "nursing" or "nourishing mother." Since colleges and other institutions of learning are supposed to nourish the minds of their students the term is applied to them.

Aloof. *Where does the word "aloof" get its meaning?*

From sailing. A strong onshore breeze may blow a sailing ship onto coastal rocks. To keep clear the helmsman must hold the vessel into the wind. The nautical term "luff" means "to the windward." Thus "to hold a-luff"— or, as we now say, "aloof"—means "to keep clear."

Alphabet. *Why do we call our ABC's the "alphabet"?*

Because the two terms are exactly the same. The Greek alphabet begins with the letters *alpha* and *beta*—whence "alphabet." Likewise, "abecederia," a name for school primers, takes its name from the first four letters of the alphabet.

Also-Ran. *How did a nonentity come to be called an "also-ran"?*

This term comes from the sporting pages of newspapers. In a horse race those entries which do not finish near the van are listed under the terse heading, "Also Ran."

Amazon. *Who gave the name "Amazon" to strong, masculine women?*

The Greeks. The word literally means "without a breast." It refers to the Grecian story of a nation of warlike women in Asia Minor. These women were such determined warriors that they burned off their right breasts in order to better draw a bow.

Ambition. *What did the word "ambition" originally mean?*

Literally "go-getting." The ancient Romans used the word *ambitio* to describe a candidate's "going about for votes."

Ambulance. *Why do we call the vehicle for moving stretcher cases an "ambulance" when walking cases are "ambulant"?*

Because the "ambulance" once brought the hospital to the patient. The French devised the term and applied it to their early field hospitals which they called *hôpitals*

16

ambulants. From this the name "ambulance" was applied to the vehicle—and it kept the name when it reversed the process and started bringing patients to the hospital.

Amen. *What is the real meaning of "Amen"?*
"Amen" is generally accepted as meaning "so be it." But in the Hebrew language, from which it comes, *amen* literally means "truly." When we use the word at the end of a prayer or hymn we assert its truth and sincerity. "Amen" is also the last word in the Bible.

Amen Corner. *How did the "Amen Corner" get its name?*
It started in England. Though today the term refers to the section of a revival meeting where the approving sit and signify their approval by interjecting frequent "Amens," it originally meant the end of a street in London. On Corpus Christi Day the priests went in procession to St. Paul's Cathedral—reciting the "Lord's Prayer" in Latin as they walked along. The prayer begins *Pater Noster*—and so the street was called "Paternoster Row." When they got to the end of the prayer they were at the end of the street and they turned the corner—"Amen Corner." As the priests turned down the lane they began chanting their *Ave Maria* or "Hail Mary"—and so the lane was called "Ave Maria Lane."

Amethyst. *What is the meaning of the word "amethyst"?*
Literally, "not intoxicating." The word is Greek and the Greeks believed that wine drunk from an "amethyst" cup was not intoxicating. Indeed, just wearing a ring with this stone in it was considered sufficient protection.

17

Ampersand. *Why do we call the "&" sign an "ampersand"?*

The old hornbooks from which children once learned their letters listed the letters of the alphabet—and ended this list with "&." The children were taught their letters by being made to recite: "A by itself A," "B by itself B," etcetera. However, they often used the Latin form. "A *per se* A," "B *per se* B," and so on. When they came to the sign for "and" they said: "And *per se* And" —and this ultimately became "ampersand." The sign "&" is merely a monogram of the Latin and Italian word for "and"—*et*.

Amuck. *Where did we get the phrase "running amuck"?*

From Malaya. Malays under the influence of opium or a stimulant sometimes become very excited—so excited that they rush about with daggers, killing anyone they chance to meet and yelling, *Amoq! Amoq!*—meaning "Kill! Kill!"

Analyze. *What is the original meaning of the word "analyze"?*

The word, which comes to us from the Greek, literally means "to loosen up." There would seem to be no connection between this and the word's present meaning, but the primitive method of gathering gold dust was "to loosen up" the earth and then toss it up into the air. Just as tossing a handful of grain into the air winnows out the chaff, so the breezes would blow away the earth—and only gold would fall back to the pan.

18

Angel. *Why do we use the phrase "to write like an angel"?*

Although "to sing like an angel" refers to celestial song, "to write like an angel" refers to Angelo Vergece, a native of Crete. In the sixteenth century he was employed by both Henri II and Francois I of France because of his beautiful handwriting.

Annie Oakley. *How did we happen to call a theater pass an "Annie Oakley"?*

Because free passes were once punched full of holes—and "Annie Oakley" was a famous rifle shot who, as a part of her act, would shoot holes in a playing card held by an assistant.

Antimacassar. *Why is a little doily on the back of a chair called an "antimacassar"?*

In the early part of the nineteenth century it was the custom for men to oil their hair. The most popular hair oil was known as "Oil of Macassar." Careful housekeepers found that a piece of cloth placed on the chair where the head rested afforded protection against oil spots on the upholstery—hence the name "antimacassar" for a chair doily.

Anxious Seat. *Where did we get the expression "anxious seat"?*

This term came into popular use in the 1820's and '30's at Methodist revival meetings. Those about to be converted were asked to "walk the sawdust trail" up to the front of the congregation where special seats were provided for them. It was the custom of the revivalist to

19

refer to the occupants of these seats as glaring examples of the evils of sin—often citing by chapter and verse their individual misdeeds. This, no doubt, is what made them "anxious"—and gave the seats their name.

Apache. *How did the "apache" of Paris come to have the same name as the American Indian?*

The French "apache" was named for the American Apache Indian by Émile Darsy—a reporter on the Paris newspaper, *La Figaro*. The term was adopted by M. Lepin, the Paris prefect of police, and so given "official" sanction. It was used to designate the gangs of rowdies who ran riot in Paris up to the outbreak of World War I. Then these gangs were rounded up and put in the front line—a simple way of eliminating most of them.

Apex. *Why is the topmost part of something called its "apex"?*

The priests of ancient Rome wore a cap which fitted close to the head; atop this cap they wore a pointed olive-wood spike; this spike was called an *apex*. Since the *apex* was the highest piece of the priest's garb we call the highest spot of anything the "apex."

Apple Cart. *What is the reason we use the phrase "upset his apple cart" to mean disaster?*

The apple cart referred to is the human body. Ever since Adam was banished from Eden, man has carried the apple (that is, original sin) within himself. And so, "to upset a man's apple cart" is to upset, not only what he is trying to do, but the man himself.

Apple of Discord. *Does the "apple of discord" refer to the apple eaten by Adam and Eve?*

No; the allusion is to Greek mythology. At the marriage between Thetis and Peleus, Discord threw a golden apple on the table, saying that it was for the most beautiful goddess there. Juno, Minerva, and Venus all claimed it. Paris was called upon to settle the point and decided in favor of Venus. Juno and Minerva felt spiteful and it was because of this, according to the story, that Troy fell.

Apple of the Eye. *Why is a loved one called "the apple of the eye"?*

The "apple of the eye" is correctly the pupil and the term "apple" probably is a corruption of "pupil"—although people originally thought the pupil of the eye was a little round ball like an apple. In any event, the allusion is to the image of the adored person so filling the pupil of the eye that nothing else can be seen.

Apple-Jack. *How did apple cider get the name "apple-jack"?*

It was once supposed that apple cider did not ripen and become properly potent until St. John's Day—June 24th; hence the names "apple-john" and "apple-jack."

Apple-Pie Order. *Why do we use the phrase "apple-pie order" to mean something extremely neat and orderly?*

Although sliced apples placed neatly one upon the other produce a neat geometric pattern, the phrase comes from the French *nappes pliées*, meaning "folded linen."

21

April Fool. *How did April 1st come to be called "April Fools' Day"?*

Up until 1564 New Year's Day in France was March 25th; but since March 25th so often fell during Holy Week the Church generally postponed its celebration to April 1st. Then New Year's Day was officially changed to January 1st—but many people still called out New Year's greetings to their friends on April 1st. Such persons were therefore "April fools"—or as the French say *"poissons d'avril"*; that is, "April fish."

Argus-Eyed. *Why do we use the expression "Argus-eyed" to describe a person who observes everything vigilantly?*

Because the mythical Argus had a hundred eyes with which to observe things. In the story, Argus was set to watch over the heifer, Io, by Juno—who suspected her husband of being too fond of the calf. Mercury finally succeeded in putting all the eyes of Argus to sleep and then slew him. Whereupon, Juno changed Argus into a peacock—and that's how it happens that the peacock has a hundred "eyes" in its tail.

Arkansas Toothpick. *What is the reason a bowie knife is called an "Arkansas toothpick"?*

It's because the natives of Arkansas were long considered by persons of surrounding states to be extremely uncouth—so uncouth that they used a bowie knife to pick their teeth.

Assassin. *How did an "assassin" get that name?*

In the year 1090 A.D. Hasan ibn-al-Sabbah formed a secret Mohammedan sect in Persia which during the Cru-

22

sades terrorized the Christians by its systematic secret murders. These murders were committed by members of the band while under the influence of hashish—and the Arabian word for a hashish eater is *hashshashin*. The ruler of this order of Assassins had absolute power over all its members and was called "The Old Man of the Mountain"—possibly from the fact that he made his headquarters on Mount Lebanon.

Auld Lang Syne. *Where did we get the expression "auld lang syne"?*

It's a Scottish phrase that literally means "old long since" —in other words, the "olden times." The song, "Auld Lang Syne," though usually attributed to Robert Burns, was not composed by him. He heard an old man singing it and took it down. The author and composer are wholly unknown.

A.W.O.L. *What do the letters "A.W.O.L." stand for?*

Since before the Civil War this term has been used in the Army to signify "Absent Without Official Leave." Confederate soldiers caught while "A.W.O.L." were made to walk about the camp carrying a sign bearing these letters.

```
B B B B B B B
B           B
B    B      B
B           B
B B B B B B B
```

Bachelor. *Why is the college degree called a "bachelor's" degree?*

Because originally a "bachelor" was a soldier not old enough or rich enough to lead his retainers into battle under his own banner. Therefore, the word meant a person of inferior rank. It was applied to the college degree in order to differentiate it from the higher degree of "doctor."

Bachelor's Button. *How did the flower known as "bachelor's button" get that name?*

The flower got its name from its similarity in appearance to the buttons on men's clothing—since these were originally covered with a rough cloth. Then, because of its name, the flower came to have significance in interpreting the chances of a bachelor with his sweetheart. If a bachelor put one of these flowers in his pocket and it did not fade but simply dried out he could hope for the best; but if it wilted and died it was a bad omen.

Back and Fill. *Why do we say an indecisive person is "backing and filling"?*

The term refers to a method of tacking a sailing ship when the tide is with the vessel and the wind against it—

in which the ship moves ahead slowly by fits and starts. The sails are allowed to "fill" with wind and then the wind is spilled from them by hauling "back" on the stays.

Back Number. *Where did we get "back number" as a name for a person who is behind the times?*

From the newspaper and magazine trade. Because each succeeding issue of a periodical bears a consecutively greater number, old copies are referred to as "back numbers."

Back Seat. *Why do we use the term "take a back seat" when referring to a lesser position?*

Because those members of the British Parliament who belong to the majority party take front seats. Those who are in the minority "take a back seat"—either of their own accord or because they are told to do so.

Back Up. *What is the reason a person who becomes stubborn and angry is said to "get his back up"?*

The allusion is to the attitude of a cat when angry—it not only raises its hair, as do most animals, but also arches its back.

Bacon. *Where did we get the expression "bringing home the bacon"?*

From country fairs. It was once the practice at fairs to grease a pig and let him loose among a number of blindfolded contestants. The man who successfully caught the greased pig could keep it—and so, of course, "bring home the bacon."

25

Badge of Poverty. *How did we come to speak of poverty having a badge—as in the expression "badge of poverty"?*

At one time in England bankrupts and beggars were compelled to wear the "dyvour" or "badge of poverty." This consisted of a coat half yellow and half brown and upper hose of the same colors.

Bags. *Why do children say "I 'bags' this"—meaning "I get it"?*

The word comes from poaching. Since whatever a poacher managed to steal would be quickly slipped into his bag—he would literally "bag" it.

Baker's Dozen. *How did 13 come to be called a "baker's dozen"?*

In the early days in England the price of bread was fixed by law. This law allowed hucksters to get thirteen batches of bread for the price of twelve. The thirteenth batch was their profit.

Bald as a Coot. *What is the reason a very bald man is said to be as "bald as a coot"?*

It's because a coot is a waterfowl with a bill that goes quite a way up the forehead—making it appear very bald.

Balk. *Why do we say we "balk" someone's efforts when we thwart them?*

Because the word "balk" comes from the Anglo-Saxon *balca*, meaning "beam"—and in the days before locks and keys a *balca* or beam was put across the door of a hut to bar enemies and thieves.

Ball. *How did a dancing party come to be called a "ball"?*

There is a Latin word *ballare* which means "to dance"—but our "ball" had its origin in the Feast of Fools at Easter. As a part of this celebration, choir-boys danced around the Dean in church; he threw a ball at them and they sang as they caught it. At early American dances, too, a ball was thrown as the dancers danced around in sets. Though they stopped throwing the ball, they kept the name, "ball" for the dance itself.

Bandbox. *What is the reason we say a neatly-dressed person looks as if he "just stepped out of a bandbox"?*

Because in the seventeenth century special boxes were made to hold the "bands" or neckpieces which men wore. These bands were light and flimsy and ruffled and quickly lost their freshness.

Bandy Words. *Why do we say we "bandy words" when we argue?*

Because there is a game called "bandy" in which the players, each with a crooked stick, beat a ball back and forth from side to side and try to get it past their opponents into the goal. To "bandy" words, therefore, is to knock them back and forth as one would bandy a ball. The phrase "keep the ball rolling" is also taken from the game of bandy.

Bankrupt. *Where did we get the term "bankrupt"?*

From Italy—where money-changers once placed the money they had to lend on a bench called a *banca*. If one of these money-changers was unable to continue in business, his counter was destroyed and so became a

27

banca rotta—since *rotta* means "broken." Because of this practice the term was applied to the money-changer himself—he was said to be a *banca rotta,* or "bankrupt."

Barber. *How did the "barber" get that name?*

At first the "barber" only trimmed beards and let the other hair alone—and the Latin word for "beard" is *barba.* When beards were shaved off and hair began to be trimmed the "barber" altered his work somewhat but kept the same name.

Bare-Faced Lie. *Why do we call a big lie "bare-faced"?*

It is easy enough to lie when you do not have to show your face—for your face may give you away. So a "bare-faced lie" is one which you make without any visible sign of compunction.

Bark Up the Wrong Tree. *What is the origin of the expression "barking up the wrong tree"?*

The allusion is to dogs trained to hunt raccoons and opossums and to leave the scent of other animals alone. They will occasionally pick up the scent of a catamount and tree it. When the hunters finally catch up with the pack they find the dogs "barking up the wrong tree."

Barnstormer. *How did actors get the name "barnstormers"?*

Actors have long been called "stormers" because of their ranting and storming. And in the early days of the theater in England there were not enough playhouses to hold all the troupes of players that toured the country. Poor troupes and those going far afield often played in barns; these players were therefore "barnstormers."

28

Batman. *Why is an Army officer's soldier-servant called a "batman"?*

Because originally it was the soldier-servant's duty to look after the pack horses—and the French word for a packsaddle is *bât*.

Bazooka. *How did the "bazooka" get that name?*

When Bob Burns, the vaudeville performer, devised a form of kazoo that had a very long sounding-horn he named it a "bazooka"—from the Dutch word *bazu* meaning "trumpet." The "kazoo"—a horn into which you sing and vibrate a little strip of paper—gets its name from the same word. The two-man rocket gun devised by the American Army during World War II was named for Burns' quasi-musical instrument because of its similarity in appearance.

Beam-Ends. *Why do we say that a person who has been knocked flat has been knocked "on his beam-ends"?*

The beams of a ship run across it, under the deck, from side to side. So, when the beams are on end the ship is turned over on its side and cannot right itself. A person who has been knocked flat is in a very similar predicament.

Bear. *For what reason is the Wall Street trader who sells stocks short called a "bear"?*

Because such a person sells stocks without having them—in the hope that the price will go down and he can purchase what he needs for delivery at a lower cost. And so the old folk saying still applies to him: "He sold the skin before he got the bear."

Beard the Lion. *What is the origin of the expression "beard the lion in his den"?*

An ancient form of insult was to walk up to a man and tug at his beard; only the weak and cowardly would stand for it. A man who would insult a lion in this manner was indeed brave; one who would attempt it in the lion's den, doubly brave.

Beat About the Bush. *Why do we say a person who avoids the issue is "beating about the bush"?*

In many forms of hunting it's necessary, in order to find the game, to follow it into the underbrush, beating the bushes and making a din to scare the animals out. A person afraid of the animals lurking there will "beat about the bush," pretending to go in to find and kill the beast—but not actually doing so.

Beaver. *Has the animal or its fur anything to do with a hat's being called a "beaver"?*

Not a thing. A hat is called a "beaver" because it is lifted off the head and at one time the portion of the helmet that could be lifted up so the wearer could take a drink was called a "beaver." This "beaver" got its name from the old Italian verb *bevere*, meaning "to drink."

Bedlam. *Why does "bedlam" mean "riotous noise"?*

Because "Bedlam" was the name of a London lunatic asylum. About the year 1247 a priory was founded in London called "St. Mary of Bethlehem." The name was soon shortened to "Bethlehem"—and then "Bedlam." Some three hundreds years later the priory was turned into a house of detention for the insane—and the wild ravings of its inmates gave "bedlam" its present meaning.

30

Beer and Skittles. *What are the skittles in the expression "life's not all beer and skittles"?*

Skittles is an old English game similar to ninepins—and since life does not consist entirely of feasting and playing, it's not all "beer and skittles."

Before the Mast. *Why do we speak of a seaman as sailing "before the mast"?*

Because a man who goes to sea as a common seaman is quartered in the forward portion of the ship—literally, "before the mast."

Behind the Eight-Ball. *What is the origin of the saying "I'm behind the eight-ball"?*

In Kelly pool little "pills" corresponding in number to the pool balls are shaken out of a leather bottle; each player in turn gets one. Allie Flint used to play this game regularly with a number of friends and liked to bet with them that he would get the lowest numbered pill. There were generally eight or more in the game and anyone who got a "pill" with a number higher than eight couldn't possibly win. Allie Flint consistently got a higher number; one day in disgust he threw down the pill exclaiming: "I never have any luck; I'm always behind the eight-ball!"

Belfry. *Does the word "belfry" come from the bells usually hung there?*

No. "Belfry" was originally the name of a military tower erected near the walls of a besieged city by the attackers so they could more easily throw their spears and shoot their arrows at the defenders. And a church steeple resembles these towers—but quite possibly the pun was appreciated by the first persons to call a steeple a "belfry."

Bell, Book, and Candle. *What is the origin of the expression "by bell, book, and candle"?*

The expression is an allusion to a ceremony of excommunication introduced into the Catholic Church in the eighth century. After reading the sentence of excommunication a bell is rung, a book closed, and a candle extinguished. From that moment the excommunicated person is excluded from the sacraments and even divine worship.

Belladonna. *How did the plant, "belladonna" get this name?*

The plant got this name because ladies once used the extract to enlarge the pupils of their eyes, and so make them beautiful. *Belladonna* is Italian for "beautiful lady."

Bellhop. *Why is a hotel porter called a "bellhop"?*

Because the desk clerk has a little bell on the counter. When he wishes a boy he rings the "bell" and the boy "hops" up to see what is wanted.

Bender. *How did a heavy drinking spree come to be called a "bender"?*

It's because the drinker "bends his elbow" every time he picks up his glass to take a drink.

Benefit of Clergy. *What is the origin of the expression "benefit of clergy"?*

The clergy was once allowed the privilege of exemption from trial by a secular court when arraigned for a felony

—and so went free. This was the original "benefit of clergy." Later this privilege was extended to any first offender who, like the clergy, could read. The test for this ability was the first verse of the Fifty-first Psalm; and so, since the ability to read it could save a man's neck, the verse was called the "neck verse."

Benny. *How did a coat come to be called a "benny"?*

In England, a common greatcoat has long been called a "Joseph"—in allusion to the "coat of many colors" worn by Joseph of the Bible. When a more stylish coat was devised by a London tailor named Benjamin, it was called, after him, a "Benjamin." From this we get "benny" and "fur benny."

Beside Himself. *Why do we describe a distraught person as being "beside himself"?*

Because the ancients believed that soul and body could part and that under great emotional stress the soul would actually leave the body. When this happened a person was "beside himself." This same thought is to be found in "out of his mind"; and in "ecstasy" too. "Ecstasy" is from the Greek and literally means "to stand out of."

Bias. *How did the word "bias" come to mean crooked?*

In bowling, a weight was once placed within the ball to make it deviate from a straight line. This was called the "bias." So, anything today which tends to make a person deviate from accepted thought or behavior is called a "bias."

33

Bigwig. *Why do we call an important person a "bigwig"?*

In Great Britain it was long the custom for all men of importance to wear special wigs. Indeed, British jurists and lawyers still wear them. So, a person of importance had a "big wig"—and was called one.

Billingsgate. *What is the origin of the term "billings-gate"?*

The firm of Lud & Billinns built a gate in the wall around the City of London that soon came to be called "Billings-gate." The London fish market was established nearby, and since the fishmongers there were noted for their loud and vulgar language "billingsgate" came to mean coarse, abusive talk.

Bitter End. *Where does the "bitter" of the expression "to the bitter end" come from?*

From the timber to which the anchor rope or chain of early sailing ships was fastened. It was called the "bitt"; and when the anchor was let out as far as the line or chain could go, it was played out "to the bitter end."

Black Maria. *What is the reason a patrol wagon is called a "black Maria"?*

The patrol wagon is supposed to have been given this name in honor of one Marie (or Maria) Lee, a negress of great size and strength, who ran a sailors' boarding house in Boston. The unruly stood in dread of her, and when the constables required help it was a common thing to send for "Black Maria"—who soon collared the culprits and led them to the lock-up.

34

Black-Out. *How did we get the term "black-out"?*

The expression was originally used in the theater—where it was applied to the extinguishing of all lights on stage while the scenery was being shifted. Then, in 1939, the British applied it to the precautionary measures they adopted to avoid revealing strategic targets for bombing to enemy German aircraft.

Black Sheep. *What is the reason "black sheep" are considered worthless?*

The wool of black sheep cannot be dyed, and so does not bring as high a price as regular wool. And yet a black sheep, though its wool has less value, eats as much and takes as much time and care as any other; therefore, it's hardly worth its keep.

Blackball. *Why do we say that a person rejected for membership by a secret society has been "blackballed"?*

Because many secret societies still follow the practice of balloting by using black and white balls dropped into the ballot box. The white stands for acceptance; the black for rejection. This custom is very old—it was used by the ancient Greeks and Romans. Even our word "ballot" means a "little ball." So, too, does the word "bullet."

Blackguard. *How did the "blackguard" get this name?*

When a noble household moved from one residence to another, the scullions and kitchen knaves traveled in the wagons with their pots and pans. Since these lowly menials were always ragged and usually extremely dirty, this portion of the train was jocularly called the "Black

Guards." Thievery was common among them and they were generally unscrupulous—thus "blackguard" came to mean a villainous person.

Blade. *What is the reason a gay young-man-about-town is called a gay "blade"?*

The Anglo-Saxon word for "branch" or "sprig" was *blaed*—and the gay and foolish young man called a "blade" was usually the young son of a nobleman—in other words, a new sprig or *blaed* of the family tree.

Blarney. *Why are soft words and sweet words called "blarney"?*

In the castle of the little village of Blarney near Cork there is an inscribed stone in a position that is difficult of access—and there is a popular saying that anyone who kisses this "Blarney stone" will ever after possess a cajoling tongue. There is, too, a legend regarding the first to ply this art. In the year 1602, Cormack Macarthy found he could no longer hold the castle of Blarney against the British and was forced to conclude an armistice by which he agreed to surrender the fort to them. But, though the British emissary, Carew received from Macarthy many soft words and sweet promises, he never got the castle.

Blimp. *How did the non-rigid balloon come to be called the "blimp"?*

When England began experimenting with this type of airship in 1914 two designs were tested—the "A-limp" and the "B-limp." The "A-limp" was unsuccessful. The "B-limp" was used and gave its name to all airships of this type.

Blind Alley. *Why is an alley closed off at one end called a "blind alley"?*

A gate or opening in a wall was at one time called an "eye." If there was no opening in the wall at the end of an alley—and so no "eye"—it was, of course, "blind."

Blind Justice. *How did justice come to be called "blind"?*

Justice is usually represented in Greek statues as wearing a blindfold and holding a pair of scales. Justice was blindfolded so she couldn't see the bribes that were being offered to her. The Egyptians carried this idea even further. They conducted their trials in a darkened chamber so that the witnesses, the pleader and the prisoner could not be seen by the judges. The Egyptians felt that this would result in an impartial decision, with no misplaced sympathy—although this system must also have resulted in an occasional misplaced prisoner.

Blind Pig. *What is the origin of the name "blind pig," often applied to a speakeasy?*

In order to get around the Massachusetts statue of 1838 limiting the sale of hard liquor, an enterprising citizen of that Commonwealth advertised that a marvelous striped pig was on view within a booth—for a small fee. Having paid the fee—which was equal to the price of a glass of rum—the spectator found within the booth a clay pig with painted stripes—and a glass of rum standing nearby. "Blind" is used in this term to indicate something "hidden" or "secret."

Blizzard. *Who invented the word "blizzard"?*

O. C. Bates, editor of the "Northern Vindicator" of Estherville, Iowa, coined, or at least popularized the

37

word "blizzard" in describing the snowstorm in Estherville on March 14, 1870. He may have had in mind the German word *blitz*, meaning "lightning"—or, from a similar root, the English dialect prefix *bliz*, meaning something "violent in action."

Bloomers. *How did "bloomers" get their name?*

Mrs. Elizabeth Miller Smith really invented the "bloomers"—but Mrs. Amelia Jenks Bloomer did so much to popularize them—both by wearing them and writing about them—that her name was given to these garments.

Blow Hot and Cold. *Why is a person who changes his mind said to "blow hot and cold"?*

When you blow with your mouth puckered up, your breath seems cold. When you do not blow as definitely, but leave the mouth flaccid, you blow hot. So, when a person starts to say something and then stops, his mouth first puckers and then becomes flaccid—and he "blows hot and cold."

Blowout. *How did a feast come to be called a "blowout"?*

A feast is called a "blowout" because it swells the paunch. Another name for such a feast is a "tuck-in"—from the double meaning of putting in the food and then having to tuck in the paunch in order to be able to wear one's clothing.

Blue Blood. *Why is a member of the aristocracy called a "blue blood"?*

Because the Spanish once had the notion that the veins in the skin of men and women of aristocratic families were bluer than those of other persons.

Blue Book. *What is the reason an official report of the British Government is called a "blue book"?*

It's because reports of the British Parliament and Privy Council are issued bound with a dark blue paper cover. A preliminary or less extensive report is issued without a cover; and so it is called a "White Paper."

Blue Laws. *How did strict, puritanical laws come to be called "blue laws"?*

The first such laws, purported to have been devised by the New Haven colonists, got the name "blue" from the adoption of blue as the color of the strict Presbyterians of the "true blue" pro-Parliament party in England.

Blue Moon. *Why do we use the expression "once in a blue moon" to mean very rarely?*

Because the phrase originally meant "never"—and a "blue moon" was supposed never to occur. But moons of blue color have been seen after certain volcanic explosions, and occasionally through smoke-laden fogs—and for this reason perhaps the phrase now means "rarely ever."

Blue Peter. *How did "hoist the blue peter" come to mean getting ready to go?*

The expression is a seafaring one. A ship about to leave port hoists a blue flag with a white square in the center—the code letter "P"—which is correctly called the "blue repeater." This stands for the French word *partir*, meaning "to depart." The flag was originally hoisted by a ship to recall seamen who had gone ashore and to give notice to the town that all with claims for money against the ship should come and make them before it departed.

39

Blue Ribbon. *Why is something special called a "blue ribbon" this or that—as a "blue ribbon" jury?*

Because an Englishman who was made a Knight of the Garter was given a blue rosette to wear at the knee; and also because the Knights of the Grand Cross, the French Order of the Holy Ghost, at one time the highest order in France, wore a blue ribbon as a badge of membership.

Blue Stocking. *Where did we get the name "blue stocking" for a female pedant?*

Indirectly, from Venice. Back in 1400 there was a society of ladies and gentlemen organized in Venice that was called *Della Calza*. This society was distinguished by the blue stockings its members wore. In 1590 the custom was introduced into Paris where women of learning adopted it. Then in 1750 a group of English women picked up the idea and formed what they called the *Bas-bleu* Club. They too, as well as the men of their circle, wore blue stockings. This created quite a scandal—since blue was originally the color of servants and others of low circumstances. The women who belonged to this group all made a point of making their conversations serious—and so today a female pedant is called a "blue stocking."

Bluenose. *How did the natives of Nova Scotia come to be called "Bluenoses"?*

A native of Nova Scotia is called a "Bluenose" because this area once exported great quantities of "bluenose" potatoes; and the potatoes were so-called because each one had a blue end—or "nose."

Blues. *Why do we call despondency "the blues"?*

Because "blue devils" were once a common form of apparition experienced by those suffering from delirium tremens or "the morning after"—though of late these imps have taken to appearing as "pink elephants."

Blurb. *What is the origin of the word "blurb"?*

When Gellette Burgess' book, "Are You a Bromide," was published, he devised a special dust jacket for some 500 presentation copies to be given away at a booksellers' banquet. Since it was then the custom to have the picture of some woman on the jacket of every novel, Burgess featured a sickly-sweet portrait of a young woman, and in the accompanying text described her as a "Miss Belinda Blurb." From this the usual dust jacket "blow up" of an author and his book came to be called a "blurb."

Bobby. *Why is a London policeman called a "bobby"?*

Because the London Police Department was organized by Sir Robert Peel. The "bobby" was taken from his first name. There is another, older term for London policemen that is not used very much now, but was at one time quite popular: "peelers"—from Sir Robert's last name.

Bobby-Soxer. *How did the "bobby-soxers" get their name?*

When young girls adopted the custom of wearing half socks they devised the name "bobby-sox" for them—since they were "bobbed" to half length. The term was then extended to the teen-agers themselves—and they became "bobby-soxers."

Body and Soul. *What is the origin of the expression "keep body and soul together"?*

It was once believed that the soul could slip out of the body rather easily. If this happened, the body could be taken over by the devil. This was very undesirable and so it was essential for everyone to "keep body and soul together." That's why we say "God bless you" when a person sneezes. The ancients believed that with a sneeze the soul was forced out of the body through the nostrils and the devil—who was lurking around every corner—would take this opportunity to slip in and block the return of the soul. If, however, a friend blessed you when you sneezed, then—because of your momentary holiness —the devil could not enter and your soul could return to your body once again.

Bolsheviki. *How did the ruling political party of Russia get the name "Bolsheviki"?*

Literally, this term just means "the greater." When the Social Democratic Party in Russia split at its convention in 1903, Lenin and his supporters—the more radical group —were in the majority and so took this name. The less radical group, being in the minority, took the name "Mensheviki"—literally "the littler."

Bombast. *What is the reason a ranting speech is said to be full of "bombast"?*

Because the soft down of the cotton plant is called "bombast" and this was much used in the sixteenth century for padding clothes. From this, padded speeches came to be called "bombast."

Bone to Pick. *Why does a person wishing to speak seriously say, "I have a bone to pick with you"?*

Two men picking over a single bone will bend their heads over, closer and closer together. Two men who are engrossed in serious conversation will do the same. In addition, if the two are disputing a point they may "growl" at each other like two dogs fighting over a bone.

Bone Up. *Where did students get the expression "bone up", meaning to study for examinations?*

From the publishing firm named Bohn which first published the "trots" which helped the students pass their Greek and Latin courses. Though the students called it "Bohn up" at first, the term was soon changed to "bone up" because of the obvious pun on "bonehead."

Bones. *Why are dice called "bones"?*

Dice are called "bones" because in play they are rattled together and sound like castanets—and castanets were once made of bones.

Boogie-Woogie. *What is the origin of the term "boogie-woogie"?*

A "boogie" is a bogie, a hobgoblin, anything magic. Witches, goblins, and other "boogies" dance to weird, disquieting music. So, music with something of the beat of the tom-toms in the bass is "boogie" music. "Woogie" is just a ricochet of "boogie."

Bookie. *How did the "bookie" get that name?*

A "bookie"—also called a "bookmaker"—carries around at all times a book in which he puts down the bets you have placed with him.

Boondoggle. *Where did the word "boondoggle" originate?*

Among Boy Scouts. The braided leather laniard worn by Boy Scouts has no real purpose. It was named a "boondoggle" by Robert H. Link of Rochester—possibly after "Daniel Boone" and "joggle." During the depression of the '30's, the name of this useless piece of equipment was transferred to the innumerable useless tasks performed by men employed on "make-work" projects of the Federal Government.

Bootlegger. *Why is a "bootlegger" called that?*

It has long been against the law to sell liquor to Indians—especially on their reservations. However, in the days when men wore high boots it was easy to smuggle in a flat pint or quart to them by slipping it into the leg of the boot.

Born to the Purple. *What is the origin of the expression "born to the purple"?*

The phrase does not refer to the purple robes worn by royalty—but to a special lying-in room designed by a Byzantine empress. The room was lined with porphyry —a purple stone—and this was the first color the children of the empress cast their eyes upon after birth.

Boss. *How did the "boss" get his name?*

From the fact that at one time he had complete authority over his workers and could thrash them at will. "Boss" comes from the Old High German *bozan* which means "to beat."

44

Boudoir. *Why is a "boudoir" called that?*

Because it is a room to which a lady may retire to sulk and pout. The term comes from the French *bouder*, meaning "to pout" or "sulk." The first boudoirs were those of the mistresses of Louis XV of France.

Bowdlerize. *What is the origin of the term "bowdlerize"?*

Dr. Thomas Bowdler edited an edition of Shakespeare, removing from it "those expressions which cannot with propriety be read aloud in the family." From this we get the term "bowdlerize" and the meaning "to emasculate by over-editing."

Boycott. *How did the word "boycott" gets its present meaning?*

The name—and its meaning—comes from the first victim of the practice. In 1880 Lord Erne, an absentee Irish landlord, employed as his agent at Lough Mask in Connemara a certain Captain Boycott. Boycott asked such unreasonable rentals from the tenants that they refused to pay anything at all. The Irish Land League adopted the practice and began using the phrase, "let's Boycott him"—meaning, "let's do it to him as we did to Captain Boycott."

Brand New. *Why do we use "brand new" to mean very new?*

Formerly the use of "brand new" was limited to things made of metal. "Brand" is an old Anglo-Saxon word which means "burn." So a horseshoe, plowshare, or sword just forged was said to be "brand new"—that is, "fresh from the fire." The term was later applied to all new things.

45

Brass Hat. *What is the reason an army officer is called a "brass hat"?*

Most high-ranking army officers have large amounts of gilt ornamentation on their caps. Since the common soldier always disparages those above him, he calls this ornamentation "brass"—and the officer, a "brass hat."

Brass Tacks. *Where did we get the expression "getting down to brass tacks"?*

From early English drapers' shops. The linen draper placed brass tacks along the inner edge of his counter and used them to measure off the material his customers wished to buy. When a woman finished looking over his stock and got down to stating the amount of cloth she wished to buy she was "getting down to brass tacks."

Break the Ice. *How did making the way easy for a person come to be called "breaking the ice"?*

Whaling ships and others sailing to Arctic regions often find ice clogging the channel through which they wish to pass—and so must send boats ahead to break the ice for them.

Bridge of Sighs. *What's the origin of the term "Bridge of Sighs"?*

In Venice a bridge connects the Palace of the Doges with the state prison and condemned prisoners on their way to execution pass over this bridge. In the center of the bridge there is a single window and prisoners frequently pause at this window to "sigh" as they catch their last glimpse of this world.

46

Bring Down the House. *Why is thunderous applause said to "bring down the house"?*

It's a bit of exaggeration. If the applause of the audience is thunderous enough and the people stamp their feet as well as clap their hands and whistle, their actions may topple a rickety theatre and literally "bring down the house."

Bromide. *Who devised the word "bromide" as a synonym for "cliché"?*

The word is an invention of Gellette Burgess. But as devised by him, "bromide" meant a man who let others do his thinking for him. In time, however, the phrase came to mean the clichés he repeated.

Brown Study. *How did we come to call a gloomy reverie a "brown study"?*

The term is the translation of the French term *sombre rêverie*. *Sombre* not only means "dull in color" but also "sad" and "gloomy." And so, "brown study" means "gloomy" or "intense thought."

Brummagem. *Where did we get the term "brummagem" as a synonym for "cheap and tawdry"?*

From Birmingham, England—which was once the great English center for the manufacture of cheap jewelry, imitation gems, and the like. "Birmingham goods" were considered inferior goods—and "Brummagem" is just a slipshod pronunciation of "Birmingham."

Bucket Shop. *Why is a "bucket shop" called that?*

In underworld slang to "bucket" is to "cheat." A firm professing to be a brokerage office, but not a member of

47

an Exchange, cannot actually place its customers' orders to buy and sell. The customers are therefore merely betting on a rise or fall in prices—and are cheated out of owning anything tangible.

Budget. *How did we get the word "budget"?*

It has long been the custom for the English Chancellor of the Exchequer to bring his papers regarding financial expenditures to the House of Commons in a leather bag or portfolio which he places on the table before him. The "budget" was named for this bag—for the Old French word for a "bag" is *bougette*. To "open the budget" is a literal description of the procedure the Chancellor follows—he opens the bag and takes out his papers.

Bull Pen. *Why is the spot where a baseball pitcher warms up called a "bull pen"?*

Although there is a ball game called "bull pen," there is every indication that the use of this term as a synonym for the spot where a relief baseball pitcher "warms up" did not come from it. Instead, the term comes from the fact that in newspaper reporting a pitcher whose delivery is hit hard and often is said to have been "slaughtered." This led to comparing pitchers with bulls and the game with a bull fight. When one pitcher was hit out of the box and another sent in, the reporters wrote, "another bull was led to the slaughter." At a bull fight there is a "bull pen" close to the arena where the bulls are kept, waiting their turn. Thus, the place where the relief pitcher warms up, waiting to be called, is named the "bull pen."

Bulldoze. *What is the origin of the term "bulldoze"?*

The term was originally "bulldose"—and meant a "dose" of whipping sufficient for a bull. It was applied in this country to the whippings the Vigilantes gave Negroes seeking office during the reconstruction period after the Civil War. The term was later applied to persons using duress—and from this idea of pushing others around "bulldoze" became associated with the machine.

Bull's-Eye. *Why is the center spot of a target called a "bull's-eye"?*

Aboard sailing ships a "bull's-eye" is an oval wooden block without a sheave but with a groove around it for the band and a hole in the center through which a small line may be drawn. A target with a center spot looks something like this block and the block looks something like an actual bull's eye—whence the name.

Bullyrag. *What is the thought behind the expression "bullyrag"?*

A "rag" is a "scold"—from the idea contained of the tongue in the expression, "wave the red rag." A "bully" is one who "bellows like a bull."

Bunk. *Where does the word "bunk" as a synonym for "nonsense" come from?*

From "buncombe." Felix Walker was the Representative in the Sixteenth Congress for the North Carolina district which included the county of Buncombe. When he made a speech in which he talked at great length about nothing of importance to Congress, the House began calling for "the question"—but Walker kept on speaking because, as he said, the people of his district expected it and he was bound and determined to "make a speech for Buncombe."

Bunk. *Why do we say a person who ducks responsibility is "doing a bunk"?*

Because a soldier anxious to get out of an unpleasant detail will pretend illness and lie abed in his "bunk."

Bus Boy. *How did a "bus boy" get that name?*

"Bus" is a shortened form of the Latin *omnibus*, meaning "for all." A "bus boy"—or "omnibus boy"—is one who does this, that, and everything, for all.

Bushwhacker. *Why is the person who lives in wild country called a "bushwhacker"?*

Because almost every person who goes in to open up new country finds it necessary to chop or "whack" out the "bushes" to make his way and create a clearing for his home.

BVD. *Where did BVD's get that name?*

For years the firm of Bradley, Voorhees & Day used the initials of the members of the firm as a trademark on the goods made for them by Erlanger Brothers. Later Erlanger Brothers purchased the trademark. Finally, the firm name was changed to the BVD Corporation—which today manufactures a full line of underwear and swim suits as well as the original "BVD's."

50

QUIZ 1

(Answers on page 266)

1. Why do we say a person in a quandary is "all at sea"?
2. How did "underhand" come to mean deceitful?
3. What is the reason we cheer on a contestant by shouting "atta boy"?
4. Why do we call the white of an egg "albumen"?
5. How did a counterman at a soda fountain come to be called a "soda jerker"?
6. Why do we say something that's very fast "goes like blazes"?
7. What is the reason a silly person is said to have "bats in the belfry"?
8. Why is an irritated person said to "bristle"?
9. What is the origin of the term "beachcomber"?
10. How did a young man or boy get the name "sprig"?
11. Why is some cloth called "broadcloth"?
12. Where did we get the expression "raise the roof"?
13. What is the reason we say a person who cannot be turned aside has "taken the bit in his teeth"?
14. Why is a domineering braggart called a "bully"?
15. Where did we get the expression "bury the hatchet"?
16. What is the word "spanking" doing in the expression "brand spanking new"?
17. Why is a large vehicle for carrying a number of people called a "bus"?
18. How did verbal hazing come to be called "ragging"?
19. Why do we say an alert person is "on the ball"?
20. What is the origin of the saying "it's in the bag"?

```
C C C C C C C
C           C
C   C       C
C           C
C C C C C C C
```

Cad. *Why do we call a vulgar person a "cad"?*

Because a page boy was once called a "cadet." For this
reason the public school boys of England called a person
who waited on them a "cadet" which they shortened to
"cad." Since these "cads" were less educated than the
schoolboys, they were presumed to be vulgar persons
devoid of the finer instincts. So, in time, any person who
possessed these attributes was called a "cad."

Calamity Jane. *What is the origin of the name "Calamity
Jane"?*

The original Calamity Jane, Mrs. Martha Burke, was a
famous western character who said she got her name
because she carried two guns and any man who trifled
with her invited calamity.

Calendar. *How did the "calendar" get its name?*

From the Latin word for an interest book kept by
money-lenders—the *calendarium*. Interest fell due on the
calends or first day of the month. *Calends* itself came
from *calare*—the Latin verb meaning "to call"—because
the Romans used to publicly "call out" the first day of
the month.

Canard. *Why do we call a lie a "canard"?*

"Canard" is the French word for "duck." And the story is told that a Frenchman named Cornelissen set out to prove the gullibility of people. He therefore reported that he had had 20 ducks but had cut up one of these and fed it to the other 19. He then cut up a second duck and fed it to those left. Then a third, and so on—until ultimately he had cut up nineteen—and all had been eaten. The story of the 20th duck that had eaten 19 others was repeated, and gave this special meaning to the word "canard."

Canary. *How did the inmate of a jail come to be called a "canary"?*

A person placed in jail was called a "jail bird" because the bars of the jail were similar to the bars of a bird's cage. He was called a "canary" because at one time English convicts sent to Australia arrived there dressed in yellow.

Canopy. *Why is a bed curtain called a "canopy"?*

The word comes to us from the Greek and literally means a "gnat curtain." The fishermen of the Nile used to sleep under a rude sort of tent made out of their fish-nets, believing—perhaps without too much foundation—that a gnat would not pass through the holes in the net.

Canter. *Where did we get the word "canter," meaning a loping trot?*

It's a shortening of "Canterbury." The pilgrims on their way to the tomb of Thomas à Becket in Canterbury rode at this speed—and so gave us the name for the gait.

53

Carat. *What is the origin of the word "carat"?*

The "carat" was originally a measure of value and not weight. And a symbol used to represent a unit of money in the time of the Roman Emperor, Constantine, looked like a picture of the fruit of the locust tree. The Arabic name for this fruit is *qirat*—whence "carat."

Carpetbagger. *Why is a scheming politician called a "carpetbagger"?*

After the Civil War in the United States many adventurers went to the South in an attempt to obtain political power by means of the Negro vote. Since most of them had little or no wealth, they carried their belongings—as well as their offices—in their handbags, generally made of carpet.

Carry Coals to Newcastle. *What is the reason a useless task is compared to "carrying coals to Newcastle"?*

It's because Newcastle is in the center of the great coal fields of England—and so it's as silly to carry coals there as to carry water to a well.

Carte Blanche. *How did we come to use the phrase "carte blanche" to mean complete freedom of choice?*

It has long been the custom for a man of importance to give a trusted subordinate blank sheets of paper or correspondence cards with his name signed at the bottom—thus giving the subordinate the right to fill in whatever he wished above the signature. Since there's no writing on the paper or card, it's a "white paper," or "white card"—in French, *carte blanche.*

Cat Out of the Bag. *What is the reason a person who divulges a secret is said to "let the cat out of the bag"?*

It's because it was once the custom for farmers to bring a suckling pig to market in a bag. Sometimes, however, a farmer would substitute a cat for the pig. If the townsman was foolish enough to buy this "pig in a poke" without first looking inside, he was cheated out of his money. But if someone "let the cat out of the bag" the deceit was uncovered.

Catch Word. *How did a "catch word" come to be called that?*

The term comes to us from the theatre. The last word of an actor's speech in the theatre is the cue word which indicates that another player is to speak. The player must "catch" this word in order to know when it's his turn. But actors probably took the term from printing—for it was once customary to print at the bottom of a page the first word of the top line of the next page.

Catgut. *What have cats got to do with "catgut"?*

Not a thing; the strings are made from sheep gut. But one name for a stringed instrument is "kit"—from the Latin name for a guitar, *cithara.* The gut strings of the instrument are therefore "kit guts." A simple wrong deduction leads to "catgut."

Cat's Cradle. *How did the children's game come to be called "cat's cradle"?*

The term was originally "cratch-cradle" and "cratch" is from the Middle English *crecche,* meaning a rack in which hay is put for cattle. The first figure created with the string in "cat's cradle" looks like a "cratch."

Cat's-Paw. *Why is a dupe called a "cat's-paw"?*

The reference is to the ancient fable of the monkey who wanted to get some roasted chestnuts from the fire. To keep from being burned he used the paw of a cat to pull them out. "Pulling one's chestnuts from the fire" refers to the same fable.

Chalk Eater. *What is the reason a man who plays the favorites at the race tracks is called a "chalk eater"?*

The term is derived from the fact that bookmakers once used to chalk their prices up on slates. A man who wished to play the favorites would pick his horse by watching the slates—and, by association of ideas, "eating the chalk."

Chancery. *Why is one of the most punishing holds in wrestling called "chancery"?*

It's a humorous reference to the English Court of Chancery which clung with tenacity and absolute control to any case brought before it, often at great cost and loss of property to the persons involved.

Charley Horse. *How did a painful stiffness of the muscles of an arm or leg come to be called a "charley horse"?*

It's sports slang. "Charley horse" is a common name for an old horse, particularly one afflicted with sweeny or other stiffness.

Chatterbox. *What is the origin of the term "chatterbox"?*

"Chatter" is, of course, an imitative word—it sounds like what it means. The "box" was added because of the similarity of sound between someone chattering and the clattering of the box used by beggars for collecting alms.

56

Chauvinism. *Why do we call exaggerated patriotism "chauvinism"?*

Because of Nicolas Chauvin, the first "chauvinist." Chauvin was a veteran of the Napoleonic wars whose patriotism and attachment to Napoleon were so exaggerated that he became ridiculous, even to his companions-in-arms.

Cheat. *Where did we get the word "cheat"?*

From English feudal law. According to this law, if the tenant died without competent heirs or was convicted of a felony his lands reverted to the lord. The term for such reversion was "escheat." To the tenant and his family this did not seem fair—and so the term "escheat" or "cheat" came to mean "dishonest practices." The word "escheat" itself comes from the Latin *excadere*, meaning "to fall to the lot of."

Checkmate. *Why is the winning move in chess called "checkmate"?*

"Checkmate" is used to describe the situation when one player in a game of chess has so maneuvered his pieces that his opponent's king cannot move without being taken from the board. The term comes from the Arabic *shāh-māt*, meaning "the king is dead."

Cheek. *What is the reason "cheek" means impudence—as in the phrase, "none of your cheek"?*

"Cheek" is here substituted for "jaw"—and your jaw is used in talking. If you stop talking you can't be impudent.

57

Cheshire Cat. *Where did we get the expression "grin like a Cheshire cat"?*

From Ireland. Cheeses once sold in Cheshire County, Ireland were molded to look like cats—and these "cheese cats" had very broad grins.

Chestnut. *How did a stale joke, come to be called a "chestnut"?*

In "The Broken Sword," a play by William Dillon, a character is forever telling the same joke about himself in connection with a cork tree. Another character says, "A chestnut tree." He insists it is a cork tree. The other replies: "Chestnut—I've heard you tell the joke twenty-seven times and I'm sure it was a chestnut." Dillon probably got the story from J. Hatton.

Chew the Rag. *Why do we say that when a person is talking he "chews the rag"?*

The "rag" is the tongue, perhaps more often called a "red rag"—as in the phrase "wave the red rag."

Chicken à la King. *What king is "chicken à la king" named for?*

King Edward VII of England—who is supposed to have ordered the dish prepared according to his own recipe.

Chicken-Hearted. *Why is a chicken considered symbolic of timidity in the phrase "chicken-hearted"?*

The reference is to baby chicks. They are very timid and run to hide under their mother's wing on the slightest provocation.

Chinaman's Chance. *What is the reason a "Chinaman's chance" is considered practically no chance at all?*

The expression became popular during those years when Californians were violently opposing the introduction of Chinese labor into the state. At that time the chances of a Chinese getting work there were very slim indeed.

Choke. *Why do we affirm the truth by saying "may I choke if this is not true"?*

Because in ancient England a person accused of a crime was given a piece of consecrated bread and cheese to eat to prove his guilt or innocence. It was believed that if the accused were guilty God would send the Angel Gabriel down to stop his throat and he would choke on the bread. Similarly, an old English test for a witch was to tie her hands and feet together and toss her into a lake. If she didn't drown she wasn't a witch.

Chow. *How did food come to be called "chow"?*

This is a pidgeon English word—it comes from "chew"—and was brought into this country by the Chinese immigrants who came to California at the time of the gold rush. Chinese restaurants still use the word in "chow mein."

Chowder. *Where does the word "chowder" come from?*

Chowder is supposed to have been invented by the housewives of Brittany. The term comes from the French word for the cauldron in which they made their chowders, *chaudière*—which in turn comes from *chaud*, meaning "hot."

59

Church Mouse. *How did a "church mouse" come to be the symbol of poverty—as in the expression, "poor as a church mouse"?*

There is no cupboard or larder in a church to produce crumbs for a mouse to feed upon.

Claptrap. *What is the reason we call cheap but showy words "claptrap"?*

This term originally meant a ruse or "trap" used by actors to induce applause or "clapping." It was an intrinsically worthless piece of business or dialogue which was showy.

Clear the Decks. *Why do we describe preparation for action as "clearing the decks"?*

It's a nautical term. Before a naval vessel goes into action, the crew members tie down or remove all movable articles on the decks so that they won't knock about and injure the sailors during the battle.

Clerk. *How did an office assistant get the name "clerk"?*

At one time only the clergy knew how to read or write—and so any person with this ability was assumed to be a "cleric." From this the words "clerical" and "cleric"—soon shortened to "clerk"—came to mean written work or one who performed such work.

Click. *Why do we say a successful endeavor "clicks"?*

Because it runs smoothly from the start. When the gears of a machine mesh immediately they go together with a single "click" instead of grinding and grating.

60

Clodhopper. *Where did the dullard get the name "clod-hopper"?*

In early England the peasants were uneducated; it was therefore assumed they were unintelligent. The gentry rode horses across the fields, while the peasantry walked afoot, hopping over the clods of earth turned up by the plow. They were literally "clodhoppers."

Clue. *How did the word "clue" come to mean a hint?*

A "clue" is literally a ball of thread—and in the old fable the only way Theseus could get out of the labyrinth was by unrolling a ball of thread as he went in.

Cock-and-Bull Story. *Where did a fanciful tale get the name "cock-and-bull story"?*

The expression is a derisive allusion to the fables of Aesop and others in which cocks moralize and bulls debate.

Cockles of the Heart. *Why do we speak of warming the "cockles of the heart"?*

The expression is redundant. "Cockle" is here used as another name for "heart"—from the fact that the cockle-shell and the heart are very much alike. Indeed, the zoological name for the "cockle" is *cardium* from *kardia*, the Greek word for "heart."

Cocktail. *How did the "cocktail" get its name?*

The father of the "cocktail" in the United States was Antoine Amédée Peychaud, an apothecary who came to New Orleans from the West Indies in 1795 and was the inventor of "Peychaud's bitters." The term "cocktail"

61

itself is probably from the French *coquetel,* the name of a mixed drink long popular in the vicinity of Bordeaux. But "cocktail" may have come from the common practice among owners of gamecocks of feeding them a special mash prepared of many ingredients—including beer or ale. This mixture was called "cock-ale."

C.O.D. *What is the origin of the expression "C.O.D."?*
In 1841, one Erastus Elmer Barclay of New York City asked William Harnden, the original express man, to deliver a package to Joseph Young in Fulton, New York. "But," Barclay said, "don't let him have it until he pays $16.50. If he can't or won't do that return the package to me. I want 'cash on delivery.' " It was another twenty years, however, before the abbreviation began to be used.

Codfish Aristocracy. *Why are the newly rich called the "codfish aristocracy"?*
The term comes from Massachusetts—where many families grew rich from its codfisheries. As the "new rich" they were looked down upon by those who had acquired their wealth at an earlier date and were derisively called "codfish aristocracy."

Cold Blood. *What is the reason a premeditated deed is said to have been done "in cold blood"?*
It was once believed that the temperature of the blood varied. When the blood became hot, a person became emotional—whence "hot-headed." When the blood was cold, reason held sway.

Cold Feet. *How did a timid person come to be said to have "cold feet"?*

It's because cases of frozen feet were frequent among soldiers until the end of the nineteenth century. And a man who has cold or frozen feet can't rush into battle. He proceeds slowly—or perhaps not at all.

Cold Shoulder. *What is the origin of the phrase expressing disinterest, "give the cold shoulder"?*

The allusion is to a shoulder of meat. A common wayfarer stopping at a farmhouse and asking for a meal would probably be given cold food. And since the common food of early England was mutton, he would be "given a cold shoulder."

Come Off the Grass. *Why do we use the expression "come off the grass" to mean "stop bragging"?*

In many large cities the parks contain little signs saying, "Keep Off the Grass." A young boy who wishes to appear smart and daring will often, therefore, walk on the grass. Whereupon his associates will probably tell him not to show so much braggadocio—by saying, "Come off the grass."

Comedy. *What is the origin of the word "comedy"?*

This word is Greek and literally means "a village singer." Greek villages once held revels at which the village bards sang songs that told a story. Out of this practice grew Greek drama and comedy.

Cop. *How did a policeman come to be called a "cop"?*

The verb "cop" means "to nab"—and a major function of the police has always been to "nab" miscreants.

Therefore, a policeman was called a "copper"—soon shortened to "cop." There is little doubt that this nickname was strengthened by the copper badges worn by the police at a later date.

Copperhead. *Where did a traitor get the name "copperhead"?*

In the Northern States during the Civil War. Copperhead snakes are as poisonous as rattlers but give no warning. So in the Civil War the Northern friends of the Confederate States were called "Copperheads"—because they often struck without warning.

Coquette. *Why do we call a flirtatious woman a "coquette"?*

Because "coquette" is the feminine form of the French *coq*, meaning a "cock" or rooster. A flirtatious woman preens herself and stresses her feminine charms much the way a cock "struts his stuff."

Corduroy. *What is the origin of the word "corduroy"?*

This is an English word that was either originally intended or soon afterwards assumed to represent a French phrase—*corde du roi*, meaning a "corded fabric of the king." But there is no such French phrase.

Corn. *Why does the word "corn" mean so many different grains?*

Because "corn" originally meant any small particle—even sand or salt. That is why beef preserved by the use of salt is called "corned beef." When "corn" finally came to mean a certain type of grain it was used to refer to the grain that was the leading crop of the locality. In

64

England, therefore, "corn" is wheat; in Scotland and Ireland, "corn" is oats; and in the United States, it's maize.

Corny. *Where did we get the slang word "corny"?*

From the ancient Sanskrit *jirna,* which means "old and worn out."

Corporation. *How did a man's large paunch come to be called his "corporation"?*

It's a humorous allusion to the belief that the men who make up the "corporation" of a town—the mayor, aldermen, and councillors—are generally prosperous and well-fed and have large stomachs. This may be because they attend so many banquets.

Cotillion. *Why is the dance called a "cotillion"?*

The word literally means "petticoat." The dance is active and the ladies who danced the "cotillion" used to hold up their dresses and show their petticoats.

Count Your Chickens. *Where does the expression "count your chickens before they're hatched" come from?*

The allusion is to the fable of the market woman who began figuring how much money she would get for her eggs. Then with this money she would buy this and that and continue to make a profit. She was still figuring her profits when she accidentally kicked over her basket of eggs and broke them.

Court Plaster. *How did an adhesive plaster come to be called a "court plaster"?*

The ladies of the courts of Europe used to cut out little patches of various shapes and sizes and plaster them on

65

their faces—to cover moles and other blemishes. From this practice "court plasters" got their name. They are sometimes improperly called "cork plasters."

Coventry. *What is the origin of the expression "sent to Coventry"?*

During the years of strife between the Kings of England and Parliament small parties of the King's men who visited the dives of Bromingham were frequently attacked and either killed or "sent to Coventry"—then strongly Protestant and pro-Parliament. In Coventry, of course, the Royalists were ostracized.

Coxcomb. *Where did a fool get the name "coxcomb"?*

From England—where professional jesters once wore a cap that in color and shape looked very much like a cock's comb.

Craps. *How did the game of dice get the name "craps"?*

The game of "craps" is an outgrowth of the game of "hazard"; and in hazard the term "crabs" was used to denote "a throw of two aces"—though no one seems to know why two aces was called "crabs." Since "crap" has long been a cant word for money, "to shoot craps"—with a *p* substituted for the *b*—came to mean "to throw dice for money."

Crazy as a Bedbug. *What is there about a bedbug that makes us say, "as crazy as a bedbug"?*

The expression owes its origin to the almost insane antics of a bedbug crawling around on a mattress. Its motions are zigzag, its direction uncertain.

66

Crestfallen. *Why do we say a disappointed person is "crestfallen"?*

The allusion is to cockfighting. A fighting cock that has won struts about with his crest red, rigid and upright. The one that has lost scurries away with his crest drooping and wilted.

Crocodile Tears. *How did false emotion get the name "crocodile tears"?*

The expression comes from what was once believed to be a fanciful tale of ancient travelers who said that the crocodile weeps over those he eats—and isn't sorry at all. But a crocodile does cry as it eats. For when a crocodile's mouth is full of food, the food presses at the top of the mouth and this releases tears from the lachrymal glands.

Crumby. *What is the reason we use the word "crumby" to mean poor quality?*

The term originally meant "very fine." It referred to the fat and fleshy part of the bread—the part which makes crumbs—as opposed to the crust. Through sarcastic use the term has acquired the opposite meaning.

Cubit. *Where does the word "cubit"—the unit of measurement so often mentioned in the Bible—come from?*

The word "cubit" is derived from *cubitus*, the Latin word for "a bend." At one time people used the arm as a measuring rod and the distance between the elbow and the tip of the second finger was called a "cubit." Under the circumstances the "cubit" varied according to the age of the individual doing the measuring and ranged from eighteen to twenty-two inches.

Curb Market. *How did the junior stock exchange in New York City come to be called the "Curb Market"?*

The men who traded in securities not listed by the New York Stock Exchange once did business on the sidewalk, street, and curb of Broad Street just below Wall Street in New York City. The traders, who had no means of communication with their office from the curb, made signs with their fingers.

Curfew. *Where does the word "curfew" come from?*

It comes from the French term *couvre feu*, meaning "cover the fire." In other words, "put out the light and go to bed."

Curiosity Killed the Cat. *What is the origin of the expression "curiosity killed the cat"?*

This expression is a corruption of "care killed the cat"—which in turn comes from the old saying that though a cat has nine lives, "care will wear them out." The change came about because a spiteful or backbiting woman is called a "cat" and women are notoriously curious. Therefore, more in hope than belief, "curiosity will kill the cat."

Curry Favor. *Why do we say a man is trying to "curry favor"?*

There is a pun intended. The Middle English word *favel* means horse; and a groom wishing to impress his master will "curry" his horse diligently.

68

```
D D D D D D
D           D
D   D       D
D           D
D D D D D D
```

D-Day. *What's the origin of the term "D-Day"?*

The "D" in "D-Day" just stands for "day"—any given day—although it is now generally used to refer to the day Allied troops invaded France in World War II— June 6, 1944. In order not to divulge the designated day of a military operation it was never written as a definite date but only as "D"; the hour was designated as "H." Other related days and hours were designated as "D+" or "D—" and "H+" and "H—."

Damocles' Sword. *How did the expression "Damocles' sword" come to represent impending danger?*

It's an allusion to an ancient legend. Dionysius the Elder was a clerk who seized the throne of Syracuse. Damocles was one of his courtiers who envied him his power and his wealth. So Dionysius invited Damocles to share his luxurious life for an evening. The two sat down to a rich banquet—but over the head of Damocles there was hung a sword suspended by a single thread. When Damocles complained that he couldn't enjoy the food at all because he was so afraid the sword would fall, Dionysius said, "Under such a threat do I enjoy my wealth and power."

Dance Attendance. *Why do we say that a person who is at another's beck and call "dances attendance" on him?*

Because according to an old wedding custom the bride on her wedding night was compelled to dance with every guest and be attentive to all of them.

Dandelion. *How did the "dandelion" get its name?*

It comes from the jagged edges of its leaves—which were supposed to look like a lion's teeth. The French form is *dent de lion*—that is, "tooth of the lion."

Dander Up. *Why do we say a man who is angry "gets his dander up"?*

When a dog or cat is angry or alarmed the hair on its back stands straight up. So too, by analogy, will a person's. And when he's thoroughly aroused, according to this humorous phrase, his dandruff will stand up too—for "dander" is merely "dandruff."

Darby and Joan. *What is the reason we refer to a loving old couple as "Darby and Joan"?*

The name comes down to us from a ballad by David Woodfall in which Darby and Joan were pictured as growing old together happily. Darby and Joan were real people: Woodfall actually served his apprenticeship with John Darby.

Dark Horse. *How did the phrase "dark horse" get its present meaning?*

At one time it was the practice among racing men for the owner of a well-known horse to dye its hair in order to get better odds. Such a horse became a "dark horse"—since you can't make horse hair lighter by dyeing it.

Davy Jones' Locker. *Where did the expression "Davy Jones' locker" come from?*

Jonah, the prophet of the Bible, was thrown into the sea. "Jones" is merely a corruption of "Jonah's." "Davy" is a corruption of the West Indian Negro's name for a "ghost" or "spirit"—*duffy*. So the phrase means "the locker of the spirit of Jonah." This, of course, is at the bottom of the sea.

Dead as a Doornail. *Why do we say something is as "dead as a doornail"?*

The doornail is the plate or knob on which the hammer of a door knocker strikes. Since this nail is knocked on the head many times a day it cannot be supposed to have much life left in it.

Dead as a Shotten Herring. *What is the origin of the expression "dead as a shotten herring"?*

Probably no other fish will die as quickly as a herring when taken out of water. A "shotten herring" is one that has just ejected its spawn—and so should die even more rapidly after being taken from the water.

Dead Heat. *Why do we call a race that results in a tie a "dead heat"?*

In trotting racing today, and at one time in almost all forms of horse racing, the horses had to run the course several times—two out of three, or three out of five wins being needed. Each of these trials was called a "heat." If two horses tied in a heat, the heat did not count—and therefore was called "dead." Today, we use "dead heat" to mean any exact tie.

71

Dead Men. *How did empty liquor bottles come to be called "dead men"?*

A pun is intended. Empty liquor bottles are called "dead men" because in both cases the "spirits" are no longer present.

Deadhead. *Why is a person riding a railroad train and paying no fare called a "deadhead"?*

The term comes from the theater. A person admitted without having to pay any admission is called a "deadhead" because he can't be counted when the revenue is figured—since the dead can't reach into their pockets to pay. The term is less appropriate when applied to railroad travel. Every corpse must have a ticket to ride a train. It must also have a live companion riding with it or pay double fare.

Deaf as an Adder. *What is the origin of the expression "deaf as an adder"?*

The basis for this simile is found in the Fifty-eighth Psalm which reads: "They are like the deaf adder that stoppeth her ear: which will not hearken to the voice of charmers, charming never so wisely." It is to be surmised, therefore, that a person "as deaf as an adder" is—or at least was originally—only as deaf as he wanted to be.

Decide. *Where does the word "decide" come from?*

The term comes from the Latin *decidere* meaning "to cut away" and one method of arriving at a decision is by "cutting away" and eliminating all but one possibility—by "cutting away" all that's worthless.

72

Delirium. *How did the word "delirium" come to have its present meaning?*

This Latin word originally meant "to go out of the furrow in plowing." But since the thoughts of a person in delirium leave the beaten track and become a jumble, they too can be said to "leave the furrow."

Delta. *What is the reason the mouth of a river is named for the Greek letter "delta"?*

All river "deltas" in the world are named after the "delta" of the Nile. This was called a "delta" because it was triangular—the same shape as the letter *delta*—Δ.

Demijohn. *Where did the jug we call a "demijohn" get its name?*

From the French. They called it a *dame-jeanne* because of its shape and wickerwork covering. The wickerwork covering seemed to give it a figure like a woman wearing an old-style corset—small at the waist but bulging above.

Derrick. *Why do we call a crane a "derrick"?*

Because a famous seventeenth century hangman of Tyburn, England was named "Derrick." Since he too hauled objects up by means of a rope and stationary arm, a crane came to be called a "derrick."

Dessert. *How did the last course of a meal come to be called "dessert"?*

The word comes from the French *desservir*, meaning "to clear the table." At one time the cloth was removed before the final sweet was served. Today, of course, we merely remove the crumbs.

Desultory. *Where do we get the word "desultory"?*

From the Roman circus. The term literally means a "rider of two horses" and the ancient Roman circus performers who rode two or more horses were wont to leap from one to the other. So a person who is inconstant and who changes his position "from one horse to another" is said to be "desultory."

Deuce. *What is the origin of the tennis term "deuce"?*

The term comes from the French *deux* which means "two." In tennis it signifies that two consecutive points are needed by either player to win.

Devil's Advocate. *Why do we say a person who questions every statement in a discussion is playing the "devil's advocate"?*

It's because when any name is proposed for canonization in the Roman Catholic Church two advocates are appointed. One of these is called "God's Advocate" and says all he can in support of the proposal; the other, "the Devil's Advocate," says all he can against it.

Devil's Luck. *What is the reason good luck is called "devil's luck"?*

To have "devil's luck" is to have good luck because it was once believed that only the devil could bring you "luck" in this world. Good people had to wait until they got to the next world for their reward. This is still believed by many.

Dexterity. *How did "dexterity" come to mean ability?*

"Dexterity" literally means "right-handedness." The person who was right-handed was assumed to be able to do

74

things with ease. The person who was left-handed would surely botch them up. For this same reason we use the French *gauche*, meaning "left-handed," to describe an awkward person. We also use the Latin word for "left,"—*sinister*. But this we have changed to mean "evil" since signs seen on the left side were said to bring ill luck, while those seen on the right brought good luck.

Dicker. *Where did the term "dicker" get the meaning "to bargain"?*

It goes back to the ancient Romans. The word is derived from *decem*, the Latin word for "ten"—and the Romans used ten hides as a basic unit in trading with the barbarian tribes.

Die Is Cast. *Is the "die" of the expression "the die is cast" the kind used in casting metal?*

No, the "die" referred to is the singular of "dice." Once you have thrown or cast the dice you can't pick them up and throw them again.

Diggings. *Where did "diggings" as a synonym for "lodgings" come from?*

This is generally supposed to be a British term for "lodgings" but it actually started during the days of the gold rush in California where each man had his own "diggings."

Dirt Cheap. *Why do we say this or that is "dirt cheap"?*

Because nothing is of less value. Should you gather a big pile of dirt you would not thereby increase your wealth; instead, you would probably have to pay someone to cart it away.

75

Distaff Side. *What is the reason women of the family tree are said to be on the "distaff side"?*

The female line of descent is so called because the women of the household once spun the thread for their weaving on the "distaff." The male line of descent is called the "spear side" because they did the fighting.

Dive. *How did "dive" come to mean a place of tawdry amusement?*

A great many of the drinking places which specialize in such amusement are located in basements below the street level—and many of their customers do not want to be seen entering them. Therefore, they "dive" in.

Do-Re-Mi-Fa-So-La-Ti-Do. *Did the syllables used for notes of the scale "do-re-mi-fa-so-la-ti-do" ever have any meaning?*

Yes. When Guido d'Arezzo invented his hexachord scale, he took the first syllables of a part of a hymn to St. John as the names of the notes—since each line of this hymn began a note higher:

> "*Ut* queant laxis
> *Re*sonare fibris
> *Mi*ra gestorum
> *Fa*muli tuorum
> *Sol*ve polluti
> *La*bii reatum."

With the invention of the octave, a name for the seventh

76

note was needed. It was taken from the initial letters of the last line of the hymn:

Sancte Iohannes.

"Do" was later substituted for "ut" because it sounded better. At an even later date, "ti" was substituted for "si" for ease in singing.

Dog Days. *Why are hot summer days called "dog days"?*

Because the ancient Romans believed that the six or eight hottest days of the summer were caused by the Dog Star, Sirius' rising with the sun and adding its heat to the day. They called these days *cuniculares dies*—"dog days."

Dog in the Manger. *Where does the expression "dog in the manger" come from?*

The allusion is to the fable of a dog who lay in the manger on top of the hay and would not let the ox or horse eat—though the dog himself could not enjoy such food.

Dogwatch. *What is the reason the late afternoon watch on board ship is called the "dogwatch"?*

The term was originally "dodgewatch" and it was created so that the same men would not have to serve the same watch day after day. Each half of the crew served a "dogwatch" between four o'clock in the afternoon and eight o'clock in the evening. It was a two-hour shift rather than a four-hour shift; and so the two groups of men changed the hours during which they were on watch from day to day.

77

Dogwood. *Where did the dogwood tree get that name?*

The tree was named for its berries and they were called "dogberries" because they were worthless—"dog" is used rather generally in plant nomenclature to denote "inferior quality" or "worthlessness."

Dominoes. *How did the game of "dominoes" come to be called that?*

The monks of a French monastery who invented it gave the game its name. The winner of the game was expected to recite the first line of the vesper service, *"Dixit Dominus, Domino Meo."* "Domino" is just a shortened form of this line.

Don't Care a Continental. *Why do we say we "don't care a continental" when we mean we care very little?*

Because during the American Revolutionary War the Continental Congress issued paper money which was practically worthless. These bills were called "continentals"—so, one who "doesn't care a continental" doesn't even care as much as that paper currency was worth.

Don't Care a Fig. *Where does the expression "don't care a fig" come from?*

The "fig" here is not the fruit but the Italian *fico* which in French is *figue.* The Italian *fico* is a contemptuous gesture made by thrusting the thumb forth between the first two fingers of the hand.

Dope. *Why is a simpleton called a "dope"?*

Because he generally acts as though he were drugged. When opium is heated it flows sluggishly and "dope" comes from *doop*, the Dutch word for a thick liquid.

Double-Cross. *Where did we get the term "double-cross"?*

From prize fighting. The fighter who intentionally loses a fight "crosses up" the spectators and those who have bet on him to win; if he wins after all he "crosses up" his manager and those who have bet on him to lose. These two "cross ups" make a "double cross."

Double Header. *What is the origin of the baseball term "double header"?*

Baseball took the term "double header" from railroading. In railroading a "double header" is a train with two engines on it. Hence, in baseball, a "double header" is two games on a single afternoon.

Double in Brass. *Why do we say someone who is versatile "doubles in brass"?*

It's an old theatrical term. Show boats, "Tom shows," and similar traveling companies generally paraded through the town before the first performance and this parade was led by a band made up of actors. Therefore, when the manager of such a company needed a new player for a minor part, he would advertise for one able to play some instrument in the band—by stating "must be able to double in brass."

Doubting Thomas. *How did a person who doesn't believe anything get the name "doubting Thomas"?*

The expression is an allusion to the Thomas of the Bible —"one of the twelve, called Didymus"—who refused to believe it was Christ who had risen from the dead until he felt the wounds.

79

Dough. *Why is money called "dough"?*

The English public school boys visit the bake shop near the school just as our children go to the ice cream parlor; there they buy cakes, pies, and puddings. The boys' nickname for these delicacies—especially pudding—is "dough." And since they spent their pocket money for "dough," they came to call the money itself "dough."

Doughboy. *What is the origin of "doughboy" as a nickname for a soldier?*

The name "doughboy" was originally applied to a small cake or dumpling fed to British sailors. They later applied it to British infantrymen—since the infantryman pipe-clayed parts of his uniform and so became covered with "dough" when it rained.

Dovetail. *How did we come to say that things which fit together well "dovetailed"?*

The allusion is to furniture making. In putting furniture together with mortar and tenon joints, the tenon is cut with a spread that looks something like a dove's tail.

Down a Peg. *Why do we say that when we have lessened a person's dignity—or popularity—we have "taken him down a peg"?*

The expression may have had its origin in the tuning of stringed instruments—but it gained meaning from a custom of the British Navy. The height of a ship's colors or flag was once regulated by the pegs to which the line was fastened on deck. The ship's colors were raised in saluting a visiting dignitary—and the higher they were

80

raised the greater the honor. So, to take the ship's colors down a peg is to decrease the honor—and to take a man "down a peg" is to lower his dignity.

Dragoon. *What is the origin of the word "dragoon"?*

The soldiers known by this name once carried short muskets. These muskets spouted fire like dragons and so the muskets were called "dragons" and the men who carried them became known as "dragoons."

Dressed to the Nines. *How did we come to say a person dressed to the utmost was "dressed to the nines"?*

The expression comes from the Old English dialect form "dressed to the eyne"—meaning "to the eyes." A person "dressed to the eyes" is "up to his (or her) ears" in clothes.

Dressing Down. *Why is a tongue-lashing called a "dressing down"?*

A butcher preparing beef for market takes a knife and slashes the animal's carcass. This is called "dressing down" the beef. Similarly, a person receiving a tongue lashing is said to receive a "dressing down."

Drink like a Fish. *What is the reason we say a person "drinks like a fish"?*

The reference is to the fact that fish swim about with their mouths open most of the time—they are therefore presumed to be continually drinking.

Drop on Him. *Where did the expression "have the drop on him" get its meaning of "have the advantage"?*

In the wild West the usual procedure in shooting a pistol is to point it at the sky and then drop the forearm

81

until the pistol points at its victim. When two pistol-toters meet the first to drop his forearm to the firing position "has the drop" on the other.

Drug on the Market. *Why do we say something no one will buy is a "drug on the market"?*

The reference here is not to drugs as we know them but to the French *drogue*, which means "rubbish"—and who would buy rubbish? Similarly, an inferior type of carpet made of scraps and leavings is called "drugget."

Drum Up Trade. *How did we get the expression "to drum up trade"?*

It was once the custom for a salesman upon reaching a town to beat a drum or ring a bell to attract the attention of the community. Having drawn a sufficient crowd, the salesman would tell the news—and sell his merchandise. From this custom we get the expression "to drum up trade"—and the name "drummer."

Drunk as a Fiddler. *What is the reason we use the phrase "drunk as a fiddler"?*

The expression refers to the fiddler at wakes and weddings whose fee was often set at "all the liquor you can hold." In order to get his full fee it was necessary for him to drink long and often.

Dry Goods. *Why are "dry goods" so called?*

Dry goods are so called to differentiate them from the goods sold by a greengrocer. The grocer sells things that are wet—or, at least, juicy.

82

Ducks and Drakes. *Where did we get the expression "playing ducks and drakes with his money"?*

From a childish game called "ducks and drakes" in which the children all toss stones—sometimes without very good aim. So anyone who throws his money about is "playing ducks and drakes" with it.

Dude. *What is the origin of the word "dude"?*

"Duds" are our clothes—from the Middle English word *dudde* meaning "to dress." The Easterner who goes West dresses himself in fancy "duds"—and to Westerners seems to pose or strike an attitude. "Dude" is "dud" plus "attitude."

Duffer. *How did the "duffer" get that name?*

"Duff" originally meant "cheat" or "fake"—and a "duffer" was a counterfeit or "no good" coin. It was in this sense of "no good" that the term was first used in respect to people.

Dukes. *Why are a person's fists called his "dukes"?*

Because the Duke of Wellington had a very large nose; therefore men with large noses were called "dukes." Then their noses were given this name. A hand doubled into a fist was therefore called a "duke buster." The "buster" was dropped and the fists became "dukes."

Dull as Dishwater. *How did we get the expression "dull as dishwater"?*

The term was not "dishwater" originally but "ditch water." Ditch water is stagnant and there isn't anything in it. Fishing in ditch water is certainly dull.

Dungaree. *Where does "dungaree" as a name for overalls come from?*

From a poverty-stricken, disreputable suburb of Bombay, India, where a coarse blue cloth is both made and worn. The name of this suburb is "Dungaree."

Dutch. *Why do we use the word "Dutch" in so many disparaging phrases?*

Because there was once a time when Great Britain and Holland were bitterly competing for foreign commerce and mastery of the sea. The British therefore used the word "Dutch" as a term of opprobrium and disparagement and to assert their own superiority. The following are typical examples of this use:

Dutch Auction.

The term refers to an auction which opens with a high bid and then works downward.

Dutch Bargain.

This phrase has two meanings—a bargain concluded over drinks and a one-sided bargain that is no bargain at all.

Dutch Concert.

The allusion is to the great noise and uproar made by a party of Dutchmen in various stages of intoxication—they sing, they quarrel, and they shout.

Dutch Courage.

By this we really mean "courage excited by drink." The British claimed that the only way the captain of a Dutch man-of-war could instill in his men sufficient courage to fight was to set up an open hogshead of brandy.

Dutch Reckoning.

When a bill that is disputed grows larger, that is "Dutch reckoning."

Dutch Treat.

No treat at all: everyone pays for himself.

Dutch Wife.

This name for a bolster was based on the presumption that Dutch women were poor bed companions—as unresponsive as the open frame bolsters used extensively in the Dutch Indies for resting the legs while in bed.

Beat the Dutch.

Only a person who told a completely incredible story could ever hope to "beat the Dutch."

In Dutch.

The phrase just means "in disgrace."

My Old Dutch.

This synonym for "wife" was coined by the famous English music-hall performer, Albert Chevalier, who explained it by the saying: "A wife's face resembles that of an old Dutch clock." But his choice of "Dutch" rather than some other nationality was undoubtedly influenced by the general use of the word for disparagement.

Dyed in the Wool. *Why do we say that someone who has very fixed ideas about something is "dyed in the wool"?*
Because when woolen cloth is dyed the color may not be even throughout; but if the dye is applied to the wool before it's spun and woven, all the cloth will be exactly the same shade.

85

QUIZ 2

(Answers on page 268)

1. *Why do we call a light sleep a "cat nap"?*
2. *Where did we get the term "chip in"?*
3. *Why is a man who undercuts established prices called a "chiseler"?*
4. *What is the origin of the word "Christmas"?*
5. *Why is a poor compliment called "left-handed"?*
6. *How did the term "cootie" come to mean a louse?*
7. *Why do we say of a glib person, "he's a corker"?*
8. *What is the origin of the term "cocksure"?*
9. *Why do we say that a girl who likes a boy "cottons up" to him?*
10. *How did an unruly lock of hair come to be called a "cowlick"?*
11. *Why do we say of an overwhelming surprise, "It knocked me into a cocked hat"?*
12. *How did the "hot dog" get that name?*
13. *Why is a great deal of money called "do-re-mi"?*
14. *What is the reason we say a person made to conform is "brought to heel"?*
15. *How did the expression "I'll be a Dutchman if I do" come to mean an unalterable decision?*
16. *What is the reason a prisoner who informs on his fellows in crime is said to "sing"?*
17. *Why do we say a brash person has "crust"?*
18. *What is the origin of the expression "I'll lead you a pretty dance"?*
19. *Why do we say something is "as dead as a smoked herring"?*
20. *Where did we get the expression "drunk as a lord"?*

```
E E E E E E
E           E
E    E      E
E           E
E E E E E E
```

Easy as A.B.C. *Why do we say that something easy is "as easy as A.B.C."?*

Because the school children of early England, given a hornbook and told to read from it, found the first part of it the easiest—for then they only had to read off the letters of the alphabet. There is no easier reading.

Easy as Duck Soup. *What is the reason we say a task is "as easy as duck soup"?*

A pond or a puddle of water is, by humorous analogy, called "duck soup." A puddle caused by rainfall will materialize without human effort. Thus "easy as duck soup" indicates a project requiring no special effort.

Easy as Pie. *Why do we say of a task that's easy to perform, "that's as easy as pie"?*

Because the full expression is, "as easy as eating pie"— and eating pie is generally considered to be a pleasant occupation that entails no trouble at all.

Eat One's Head Off. *What is the reason we say a lazy person "eats his head off"?*

The expression was originally applied to horses whose food cost more than they could earn. It refers to the humorous notion that a horse eating oats will keep on nibbling its lips after the oats are gone and, if not stopped, will finally succeed in eating its own head off.

Eavesdropper. *How did we get the term "eavesdropper"?*
In Saxon times in England the owners of estates could not build their homes or cultivate their land right up to the property line. They had to leave a little space for the drip from the eaves. This space soon came to be called, from that fact, the "eavesdrip." An "eavesdropper" was a person who placed himself in the "eavesdrip" to overhear what was being said.

Economy. *Where does the word "economy" come from?*
From the Greek word for "house manager." The one place where we generally insist on the careful expenditure of money is in our own home.

Electricity. *Who invented the word "electricity"?*
Dr. William Gilbert—who became physician to Queen Elizabeth in 1601. Dr. Gilbert gave the name "electric" to static electricity produced by rubbing a piece of amber with a cloth. He derived the name from *elektron,* the Greek word for "amber."

Eleven, Twelve, Thirteen. *How did the numbers "eleven" and "twelve" and the "teens" get their names?*
"Eleven" comes from "leave one"—you count the ten fingers and that leaves one. Twelve is "twa" or "two left." Thirteen is "three plus ten."

Etiquette. *What is the origin of the word "etiquette"?*
At one time visitors to the court of France who might not know how to behave properly were given a card of

88

instructions—a sort of ticket. From this the French devised the term "etiquette" and applied it to all rules of social behavior.

Examine. *How did we come to use the word "examine" to mean "test"?*

An old fashioned balance scale has a little indicator which shows which tray outbalances the other. This indicator was called in Latin an *examen*. Thus, to "examine" is to watch this indicator and, by analogy, "weigh in the balance."

Exception Proves the Rule. *What is the origin of the expression "the exception proves the rule"?*

Orginially the word "prove" meant "test." And so, the phrase merely means that the "exception tests the rule." In this sense the saying is quite logical.

Exchequer. *Where did the word "exchequer" come from?*

From *eschequier*, the Old French word for a chess or checker board. During the time of Edward I of England a special court took care of the King's revenues. A cloth-covered table was used by this court and the cloth was checkered—so the court was referred to as the "Exchequer."

Eye and Betty Martin. *Why do we use the expression "all my eye and Betty Martin" to mean nonsense?*

The expression owes its popularity to a story that had wide circulation. A British sailor went into a foreign church where he heard the priest uttering these words: *Ah, mihi, beate Martine* ("Ah, grant me, Blessed Martin"). In telling of his experience the sailor said, "And

89

all the sense the fellow ever made was when he said 'All my eye and Betty Martin'."

Eye of a Needle. *What is the reason we say that something is as difficult as "for a camel to pass through the eye of a needle"?*

The expression comes from the Bible. "The needle's eye" was a name given to a small gateway built in the Wall of Jerusalem for the use of pedestrians. A small camel could actually work its way through this gate—if it kneeled down and struggled hard—but it would be very difficult.

```
F F F F F F
F            F
F      F     F
F            F
F F F F F F
```

Faction. *Where did we get the word "faction"?*

From the Romans. The charioteers who performed in the Circus Maximus were divided into four different parties and the Latin word for "party" is *factio*. Each "faction" wore a different color and originally represented a different season of the year—although with time the number of "factions" was increased to six. Civil war between the "blue faction" and the "green faction" in 532 A.D. led to the current meaning of "opposing political groups."

Fall Guy. *Why do we call a dupe a "fall guy"?*

The word "fall" not only means to "stumble" but also to be "lured" or "entrapped." And so we call a person a "fall guy" who is entrapped and left to suffer the punishment while the one who did the actual mischief escapes.

Farce. *How did the word "farce" come to mean "comedy"?*

"Farce" comes from the Latin *farcire*, meaning "to stuff." The early miracle plays were padded or stuffed with jokes and low comedy scenes—and so this type of comedy came to be called "farce."

Fast and Loose. *What is the reason a person indulging in trickery is said to be playing "fast and loose"?*

"Fast and loose" was the name of one of the "skin games" played at fairs in England in the Middle Ages. The trickster folded a belt and then asked a player to pin it fast to the table with a skewer. After the player had done this the trickster suggested a bet. Then he loosed the belt and showed it to all, showing them that it had not been pierced by the skewer anywhere.

Fat's in the Fire. *Why do we say "the fat's in the fire" when we mean there's trouble ahead?*

Because when the fat in the frying pan is spilt into the fire the flames leap up and can burn you.

Feather in His Cap. *Where did we get the expression "a feather in his cap"?*

The American Indian who added a new feather to his headgear for every enemy slain was the father of this phrase. The same procedure has been followed by many other races and nations.

Fiasco. *How did a complete failure come to be called a "fiasco"?*

The making of a fine Venetian glass bottle is a difficult process—for it must be perfect. If, in blowing, the slightest flaw is detected the glassblower turns the bottle into a common flask—called in Italian, *fiasco*.

Fiddlesticks. *Why do we use the exclamation "fiddlesticks"?*

In the eyes of the serious-minded to "fiddle" is to waste time—as in the term "fiddling around." The fiddle is

92

therefore a worthless object. Since the bow or "fiddle-stick" is even less important to fiddling than the fiddle itself, "fiddlesticks" means of no worth whatsoever.

Fifth Column. *What is the origin of the term "fifth column"?*

This phrase was coined by the Spanish Fascist General, Emilio Mola. While Franco forces were besieging the city of Madrid, Mola made a special broadcast to the Loyalists defending the city in which he stated: "Four of our columns are marching upon your city and at the appropriate time a 'fifth column' behind your own lines will arise to the attack."

Filibuster. *How did we get the name "filibuster" for legislative obstruction?*

Since the Spanish called a freebooting pirate out to get what he could for himself a *filibustero*, a legislator with similar ideas was given this name. The usual method employed for this purpose by the legislator was to obstruct the passage of all bills until his demands had been met. So today any legislator who obstructs legislative procedure is said to "filibuster."

Fine Italian Hand. *Why do we use the expression "fine Italian hand"?*

This phrase has a double meaning. In the fifteenth century Italian penmanship was exceedingly fine and ornate; at the same time the court politicians of Italy were exceedingly sly—and so the term was used to mean "sly manipulation covered by beautiful appearance."

93

Fire and Water. *How did we come to say a person who suffers trial and tribulations "goes through fire and water"?*

It's because in early times a method of proving one's innocence was to suffer trial by ordeal. One ordeal was by fire; the person either walked barefooted and blindfolded through hot coals or carried a red-hot iron bar for a distance. Another ordeal was by water; the person plunged his hand into a pot of boiling water.

Firedogs. *Why do we call andirons "firedogs"?*

Because at one time real "dogs" were placed in a wheel-cage at one end of a roasting spit and had to run round and round the wheel to turn the spit. Sometimes a live coal was placed inside the wheel to speed up the dogs.

First Blush. *What is the reason the phrase "at first blush" means without full consideration?*

Because it's to be presumed that the first time a young lady is presented with a proposition—either honorable or dishonorable—she will naturally blush. So, "at first blush" means immediately and without any previous consideration.

Fit in the Arm. *How did we come to call a blow by the fist a "fit in the arm"?*

This synonym for a "punch" had its origin in a remark made in court. One Tom Jelly, a resident of the London slums, was arrested for striking a woman. His defense was that "a fit had seized him in the arm." This was just too good for the general populace to miss. The term was quickly picked up and widely used.

94

Fit as a Fiddle. *What is the reason we say someone is "fit as a fiddle"?*

The phrase originally was "fit as a fiddler" and referred to the stamina of fiddlers—who could play for a dance all night long without ever getting tired.

Fix. *Why do we say a person in trouble is in a "fix"?*

Because when machinery won't work, it's in need of "fixing"—or, by shortening the phrase, "in a fix." The same term is applied to persons who need "fixing" or help of some kind.

Fizzle. *Where does the word "fizzle" come from?*

It's just a vocal imitation of the sound of the fuse of a cannon that splutters and goes out—"f-z-z-z." Whence both "fizz" and "fizzle."

Flak. *What is the origin of the word "flak"?*

It's a contracted form of the German *"Fliegerabwehr-kanonen"*—meaning "anti-aircraft gun." Since Allied airmen came more closely in contact with its missiles than the gun itself they used "flak" to mean the barrage the gun sent up.

Flame. *How did the word "flame" come to mean the object of our affections?*

Just as in our popular songs "June" is always used to rhyme with "moon," the common rhyme of the French classics is *flamme* and *âme*. So we call the loved one (*âme*) a "flame" (*flamme*).

Flapper. *Why do we call a young girl a "flapper"?*

Because a fledgling wild duck flaps its wings but cannot fly. A young girl is said to be a "flapper" when she at-

95

tempts to act like a woman but is not yet one. The term is very old and at first was applied only to girls too young to conceive.

Flash in the Pan. *How did we get the expression "flash in the pan"?*

The old flintlock type of gun had a "pan" on which a little trail of powder led from the charge in the gun to the flint. When the hammer struck the flint and ignited this trail of powder but the gun did not go off—then it was just a "flash in the pan."

Fleshpots. *What is the reason carnal desire is called "hunger after the fleshpots"?*

"Fleshpots" were originally just those pots in which the flesh of animals was cooked—and "to hunger after the fleshpots" was to want a good meal of meat. Only by analogy did the flesh become human.

Flibbertigibbet. *How did the word "flibbertigibbet" come to mean a chatterer?*

By the addition of several unnecessary onomatopoeic syllables to make the meaning doubly clear. "Gib" is no doubt a variant of "gob" which means "mouth"; "flibber" is an echoic variant of "flutter." So a flibbertigibbet is a "flutter-mouth."

Flivver. *Where does the term "flivver" come from?*

From a confused blending of "flopper" and "fizzler." The use of "flivver" to refer to automobiles still has a slightly derogatory meaning.

Flush. *What is the reason a man with money in his pocket is said to be "flush"?*

Because a beaker or other container filled to the top is filled "flush." Likewise, a person's pocket filled to the top with money is "flush"—and so is he.

Fly Off the Handle. *Why do we say a person "flies off the handle" when he gives vent to his anger?*

The expression refers to the head of an ax. A wood-chopper giving vent to his anger will chop so violently that the head of the ax will "fly off the handle."

Fly a Kite. *How did the expression "go fly a kite" originate?*

In England, many years ago, a person who sent begging letters to men of prominence whom he knew only by name—in a general sort of hope that some one of them might come to his rescue—was said to be "flying kites." The expression was prompted by the fact that you can, by "flying a kite," see how the wind is blowing. So, to tell a person to "go fly a kite" was the equivalent of saying: "Ask someone else—not me." Later, the meaning became "go play by yourself"—and from this comes the use of the term as a euphemism for a far more vulgar and common expression.

Flying Dutchman. *What is the reason a vessel vaguely seen passing in a fog is called a "flying Dutchman"?*

According to legend, the "Flying Dutchman" was a vessel which started to round the Cape of Good Hope during a bad storm. When the crew became frightened and mutinied, the captain put the ringleaders to death. Then the Holy Ghost, in the form of St. Elmo's light, appeared

97

at the masthead and told the captain to desist. He answered by drawing his pistol and firing at the light—but the pistol exploded in his hand and paralyzed his arm. The captain was wild with rage; he cursed and swore he would continue to round the Cape against the wind if it took him until the "crack of doom." The Creator took him at his word—and ever since then the ship may be seen sailing against the wind in a vain attempt to double the Cape of Good Hope.

Fogey. *How did a man who is "behind the times" come to be called an old "fogey"?*

There was once a standard English word, "foggy," which meant "fat" or "bloated" or "moss-grown." The Scottish adopted the word as "fogey" and used it as a disrespectful name for an old man who was "behind the times."

Fond. *What is the reason we say a "fond" mother "fondles" her child?*

Because both terms come from the Middle English word *fon*, meaning "foolish." A "fond" mother "fondling" her child is likely to do all sorts of foolish things.

Fool. *Why do we call a jester a "fool"?*

Because he makes faces and puffs out his cheeks. He's a "windbag" too. *Follis* is the Latin word for "windbag" and *folles* refers to his puffed-out cheeks.

Four-in-Hand. *What is the reason "four-in-hand" is used to describe both a kind of coach and a kind of tie?*

The coach is drawn by four horses and all the reins are held by one person—in just one hand if he's wielding the

98

whip with the other. The ends of the tie hang from the throat in a manner similar in appearance to the reins falling down from the hand of the four-in-hand driver.

Frank Merriwell Finish. *Where does the expression "a Frank Merriwell finish" come from?*

From a series of books popular at the turn of the century. Frank Merriwell, the hero of these books, was always getting into very difficult situations but, after overcoming many unbelievable obstacles, always came out on top. So today, a "Frank Merriwell finish" is one achieved by overcoming great difficulties with a great deal of accompanying excitement.

Free Lance. *Why is an independent writer, photographer, or the like called a "free lance"?*

A medieval mercenary soldier who was free of any continuing loyalties was known as a "free companion." Sir Walter Scott in his novel, "Ivanhoe," coined a more descriptive term for such a soldier—"free lance."

Freedom Suit. *What is the origin of the term "freedom suit"?*

In Colonial times men of means in this country paid for the passage of Europeans who wished to come to the New World; they exacted, in return, a period of indentured service. At the end of this period of servitude the master gave his indentured servant a "freedom suit" which followed the style of the period and had none of the distinguishing features of the livery previously provided.

99

French Leave. *How did leave without permission come to be called "French leave"?*

"French" is used in this term in a derogatory sense that is quite often found in English expressions. The French return the compliment. Anything either believes to be unworthy is credited to the other.

Frog. *Why is a Frenchman called a "frog"?*

Because the shield of Paris has frogs upon it and because Frenchmen eat frogs—which the uneducated English once considered very queer indeed.

Full of Beans. *How did we come to use the term "full of beans" to describe an active and energetic person?*

Beans have long been considered the one food sure to produce energy. Therefore, a person who is active and energetic must be "full of beans."

Full Blast. *Why do we add the word "blast" to "full" in order to mean the utmost—as in the phrase "going full blast"?*

Furnaces in steel plants use a forced draft that is called a "blast"—and the furnace is called a "blast furnace." When in full operation the furnace is "going full blast."

Funny-Bone. *What is the reason the spot at our elbow is called a "funny-bone"?*

It's a pun. This spot not only gives us a "funny feeling" when we hit it; it's also located at the enlarged end of the bone known to medical science as the "humerus."

QUIZ 3

(*Answers on page 270*)

1. *Why do we say a person who takes care of himself "feathers his own nest"?*
2. *What is the origin of the expression "fair-weather friends"?*
3. *How did a "fortnight" come to be so called?*
4. *Why do we call motion pictures "the flickers"?*
5. *What is the reason we call a person we admire a "good egg"?*
6. *How did the sports "fan" get that name?*
7. *Why do we say "fork over" when we mean "hand over"?*
8. *What is the relationship between the words "edifice" and "edify"?*
9. *Why is a comedian's stooge said to act as his "foil"?*
10. *How did "like fun" come to mean "no"?*
11. *What is the origin of the term "Good Friday"?*
12. *Where did we get the expression "playing both ends against the middle"?*
13. *Why is a miserly person said to "make the eagle scream"?*
14. *What is the origin of the word "twenty"?*
15. *Why do we say a person who has not made up his mind is "on the fence"?*
16. *How did we come to call a suspicious proposition "fishy"?*
17. *Where did we get the term "foot-loose"?*
18. *Why do we say a gay, carefree person is "devil-may-care"?*
19. *What is the reason fingers, toes and numerals are all called "digits"?*
20. *How did we get the expression "all fagged out"?*

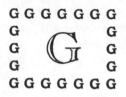

Ga-Ga. *Why do we say a person in love is "ga-ga" over the object of his affections?*

Because a person may be so struck with love that his mouth falls open and the only sounds that come out are "ga-ga-ga."

Gag. *How did a joke come to be called a "gag"?*

The term was originally used by actors to mean an ad-lib joke thrown in to throw another actor off his lines. The joke stopped his speech as effectively as a gag.

Gamut. *Why do we say a person "runs the gamut" of emotions?*

Because "gamma" represented the last note on Guido d'Arezzo's musical scale and "ut" represented the first note used in his singing scale. So, to "run the gamut" has come to mean to run the entire scale of emotions—no matter how represented.

Gandy Dancers. *What is the reason the men who pump a railroad handcar are called "gandy dancers"?*

The men who pump a railroad handcar are usually four in number and they stand in positions similar to the two couples of a square dance. Their deep knee-bending as they work the car suggests such a dance performed by geese—or more exactly, "ganders."

Garble. *Where does the word "garble" come from?*

From the Arabic word for "sieve"—*ghirbāl*. At first "garble" meant "to sort out" and was applied to the selection and sorting out of individual passages from a man's writings. But the persons who made the excerpts often edited and changed the context considerably; and so "garbled" came to mean "mixed up and mutilated."

Gargoyle. *Does the word "gargoyle" refer to the appearance of these images?*

No. "Gargoyle" is an Old French word and literally means "throat." Gargoyles were originally used as projections from the gutter of a building to carry the rainwater clear of the walls, and they spurted this drain water through their "throats."

Garrison Finish. *Where does the expression "garrison finish" come from?*

From horse racing. A jockey named Garrison made it his practice to hold his horse back until the last minute in order to come from behind to win.

Gat. *How did we come to call a revolver a "gat"?*

The name "gat" was originally applied to a machine gun invented by Dr. Robert Gatling and first used during the Civil War. But this gun had a cluster of ten barrels that looked something like the chamber of a revolver—and so the name was transferred to the revolver.

Gee-Gee. *Why are horses called "gee-gees"?*

Because in earlier days horses were urged on by their drivers with the phrase "gee-up, gee-up"—instead of "giddyap." Little children shortened the command to "gee" and introduced "gee-gee" as a synonym for the horse itself. Racing men adopted the term from this childish use.

Geronimo. *What is the reason American paratroopers shout "Geronimo!" as they jump?*

Several members of the first unit of parachute troops formed at Fort Benning, Georgia went to see the motion picture "Geronimo." Afterwards, in derisive reference to the mock heroics of their practice jumps, they started calling each other by this name. From this grew the paratrooper's practice of shouting "Geronimo" as he leaps from the plane.

Gerrymander. *How did we get the word "gerrymander"?*

Elbridge Gerry, a Democrat, was Governor of Massachusetts in 1812 and had a Democratic legislature serving with him. In order to secure increased representation in the State Senate they redistributed the state, dividing it up so that the Federalist minority would not be able to elect a true percentage of the legislature. As a result of this a district in Essex County was formed with a very irregular outline. Benjamin Russell, editor of the "Columbian Centinel," hung a map of the new districts in his office. Gilbert Stuart, the painter, saw this map and noticed the peculiar outline of the district in Essex County; he added a head, wings, and claws to it and exclaimed: "That will do for a salamander." "No," said Russell, "Gerrymander." Thus, to redistribute a state to get the maximum possible representation for one party at the expense of the other came to be called "gerrymandering."

Get One's Goat. *Where does the term "get his goat" come from?*

From horse racing. Racing men will often place a goat in the stall with a nervous race horse. The horse soon becomes accustomed to having a goat there and finds it very comforting; he becomes less nervous and is not so easily upset. If, however, the owner of a rival horse can steal or "get" this goat, then the horse is even more nervous than before and may lose the race.

Ghost Walks. *Why do we use the expression "the ghost walks today" to mean it's payday?*

Because of a theatrical anecdote. There once was a company of English strolling players who had been unpaid for some time. During a rehearsal when Hamlet said, in reference to the ghost. "Perchance 'twill walk again," the "ghost" answered, "No, I'll be hanged if the ghost walks again until our salaries are paid."

G.I. *How did American soldiers get the nickname "G.I."?*

"G.I." stands for "Government Issue," and the term was originally applied only to those articles which were actually issued by the government. But in army slang it now means practically everything in army life that is standardized, orderly or regimented—including the soldiers themselves.

Gift Horse. *What is the reason we say "never look a gift horse in the mouth"?*

It's because the value of a horse is determined primarily by its age; and the age of a horse is determined by looking at its teeth. You should not question the value of something that is given you—and you won't if you "never look a gift horse in the mouth."

Gingerbread. *Why do we call fancy scroll work and gilt decorations "gingerbread"?*

Because at one time very fancy gingerbread animals sold at fairs were elaborately decorated with gilt or gold leaf.

Go to Pot. *What is the reason we say of something that's deteriorated "it's gone to pot"?*

It's because smiths generally keep a pot on hand into which they throw broken pieces of the metal on which they are working. These scraps are ultimately melted down and used again. Anything which has no further use goes into this pot.

Go West. *How did the term "go west" come to be used as a synonym for death?*

In the beginning this expression did not mean "to die" but just "to disappear from sight." In the early days of our country many men who were wanted for a crime in the East "went out West" into the wilderness. Some lived; some died; but all who wished to do so disappeared from sight. But since they "might as well be dead" the term in time came to mean death.

106

God Bless the Duke of Argyle. *What is the origin of the saying, "God bless the Duke of Argyle"?*

It's an old Scottish expression of gratitude to the Duke of Argyle for setting up a line of guideposts to help his herdsmen find the trail when the ground was covered with snow. The herdsmen, however, blessed him for these posts in all weather—because they could rub their backs against them when they felt somewhat itchy. It was once the custom to remark, "God bless the Duke of Argyle" to relieve the embarrassment of a guest caught backing up to a post with a wistful wiggle.

Gone 'Coon. *How did we get the expression "a gone 'coon"?*

The reference here is to a famous story—often told of Davy Crockett, who was an expert shot. Out hunting, Crockett leveled his gun at a tree in which a raccoon was concealed. Knowing Crockett's prowess with a gun the 'coon called out, "Are you Davy Crockett? If you are, I'll just come down out of this tree 'cause I know I'm a gone 'coon."

Good Footing. *Where does the expression "he's on a good footing with his boss" come from?*

From the fact that during the reign of King Henry VIII of England the size of a man's shoe indicated his rank. The man who was unimportant wore a small shoe; the man who was important wore a large shoe to indicate that he was in good standing—"on a good footing" with the King.

Goose Hangs High. *Why do we say "the goose hangs high" when we wish to express the idea that everything is fine?*

This phrase, though its origin is obscure, is probably a corruption of "the goose honks high." Wild geese "honk" as they fly—and the height at which they travel is determined by the weather. In stormy weather they fly close to the earth; in fine weather they travel—and "honk"—high.

Goose Step. *What is the origin of the term "goose step"?*

The name "goose step" was originally applied to a British setting-up exercise in which a new recruit was made to stand on one leg and swing the other backward and forward without bending the knee—just as a goose stands on one leg and swings the other. Because of a similarity of appearance—in particular, the straightened knee—the term was applied to the German military march step in which the foot is raised sufficiently to give it a twenty-inch stride.

Gordian Knot. *How did a great difficulty come to be called a "Gordian knot"?*

This expression grew out of a legend about the Phrygian king, Gordius. Gordius was a peasant who, upon being chosen king, dedicated his wagon to Jupiter and then tied the yoke to a beam with a rope made of bark. The knot was so ingeniously tied that no one could untie it; it was said that whoever did so would reign over the whole East. Alexander the Great was shown the knot and told the story. "Well, then," said he, "this is how I do it"—and with his sword he cut the knot in two.

Gossip. *Where did the word "gossip" come from?*

In early times a godparent of a child was called a *God-sibb—sibb* meaning "related." Since godparents were usually chosen from among distant relatives who met only at rare intervals, there was sure to be a great exchange of news and small talk at the christening. This led to the general belief that *god-sibbs* were idle chatterers—and to the adoption of their name as a synonym for idle talk.

Gout. *What is the origin of the word "gout"?*

"Gout" comes from the French *goutte* and literally means "drop." This disease was once supposed to be caused by the blood's "dropping" morbid material in and around the joints.

Grandfather Clock. *How did the "grandfather clock" get that name?*

The name comes from a popular song of the 1880's which began:
"My grandfather's clock was too tall for the shelf
So it stood ninety years on the floor. . . ."

Grapefruit. *Is there any reason why "grape" is used in preference to another fruit in the word "grapefruit"?*

Yes—grapefruit grows on the trees in clusters like grapes.

Grapevine. *Why do we say a rumor travels via "grapevine"?*

The term is a shortened form of "grapevine telegraph." In 1859 Colonel Bernard Bee constructed a telegraph line between Placerville and Virginia City by attaching the wire to trees. With time the wire—no longer taut—lay on the ground in loops that looked a lot like wild, trailing grapevine. During the Civil War similar lines were used by the troops and since the reports which came in over such "grapevine telegraph" lines were more often than not conflicting, the term "grapevine" was used to refer to widespread rumors which had no definite source and were generally false.

Grass Widow. *What is the origin of the term "grass widow"?*

In the days before divorces the only proper husbandless mother of a child was a widow, while a girl who took up prostitution as a profession was said by country folk to have "gone on the turf" or "gone on the grass." If such a girl became the mother of a child she would naturally claim to be a widow—although "wed in the grass and widowed there."

Great Shakes. *How did we come to say something of little importance is "no great shakes"?*

The term comes from shooting dice. If you "shake" and throw a losing number, it's certainly "no great shakes."

Greek Meets Greek. *Where did we get the expression "when Greek meets Greek"?*

The reference is to the wars of Alexander. Alexander of Macedonia set out to conquer the other states of Greece but each city in turn offered him obstinate resistance. An early play about Alexander the Great contains the line: "When Greeks joined Greeks then was the tug of war."

110

Greeks Had a Word for It. *Why do we say "the Greeks had a word for it"?*

Because the words of classical Greek had many forms— a fully conjugated verb possessing several hundred. This variety of word-forms made possible a precision in expression not attained in most ancient languages and many modern ones.

Greenhorn. *How did we come to call an inexperienced person a "greenhorn"?*

The word was first applied to a young ox with new horns. By analogy these new horns were "green." (In this sense "greenhorn" was used as long ago as 1460.) Since a person who does not know his way about is like a young or "greenhorn" ox that doesn't know which way to turn when you shout "gee" or "haw" at it, the term "greenhorn" has been applied to the person.

Gretna Green Marriage. *Where is the "Gretna Green" of the term "Gretna Green marriage"?*

In Scotland. Although England has long had rather strict marriage laws, at one time Scotland did not. All the marriage ceremony needed in Scotland was a mutual declaration by the two elopers in front of witnesses. So, the English boys and girls went to Scotland to be married in a hurry—and to Gretna Green in particular, since it was the most accessible spot. There they had only to declare their intent to become legally married without license, banns, or priest.

Grocer. *What is the origin of the word "grocer"?*

The word "grocer" originally meant a "wholesaler." The English merchant who dealt in spices, dried fruits, tea, coffee, and such foodstuffs in retail amounts was called a "spicer." A wholesale dealer in these articles was called a "spicer en gross"—or a "grosser"—since he sold goods in bulk and by the gross. The word "gross" is from the French *gros* meaning "great" or "large."

Grog. *Why is the rum served on British Navy ships called "grog"?*

Because Admiral Edward Vernon of the British Navy was nicknamed "Old Grog"—in reference to the grogram cloak he always wore. As an economy measure, Vernon introduced into the Navy the custom of serving rum mixed with water instead of "straight" rum. This mixture was called "grog" in his honor—and the name stuck.

Grundy. *How did a woman who sets the fashion for her neighbors get the name "Mrs. Grundy"?*

The name comes from the play by Tom Morton called "Speed the Plough." One of the women characters in the play is so concerned over the reactions of her neighbor, Mrs. Grundy, that her husband finally exclaims: "Be quiet. All this ding, dinging Dame Grundy into my ears. What will Mrs. Grundy say—what will Mrs. Grundy think?"

Gunny Sack. *Why is a "gunny sack" called that?*

"Gunny" is an Anglicized form of the Hindu and Sanskrit word *goni* which simply means "sack" or "bag." Because the coarse, heavy sacking and the bags themselves were once made on a large scale in Bengal, the material itself came to be called "gunny" and the bags became "gunny sacks."

Guy. *What is the reason the word "guy" is used to mean a man?*

The English use "guy" to signify a grotesque and ludicrous person—in allusion to Guy Fawkes, a leader of the "Gunpowder Plot" of 1605, and the effigies of him strung up on street corners on November 5th. The American term is derived from the "guy" rope of a circus tent—in such phrases as, "Who's the 'main guy' here?"

Gymnastics. *Where did we get the word "gymnastics"?*

The word comes to us from the Greek *gumnos*, which means "naked." From this the Greeks devised the word *gymnasium* to denote a public place for athletic sports. The athletes of early Greece removed their clothes to compete with one another.

Gyp. *Why do we call a trickster a "gyp"?*

The word comes from the Greek and literally means "vulture." Students at the University of Cambridge applied the name to the servants furnished them by the college, since these servants found innumerable ways of obtaining tips from them and so, by implication, preyed upon them like vultures. From Cambridge the word went into general use—a person who was not quite honest and his method of acquiring things by trickery both being called a "gyp."

Gypsy. *How did the "Gypsies" get their name?*

The Gypsies claim Egypt as their original native land and their name is derived from "Egypt." But it is far more likely that they originally came from India in the Middle Ages—and merely passed through Egypt on their way into Europe.

```
H H H H H
H         H
H    H    H
H         H
H H H H H
```

Hair of the Dog. *Why is taking a morning-after drink as a pickup called taking a "hair of the dog that bit you"?*

Because the ancients believed that one of the best cures for hydrophobia, or any other disease you might obtain from a dog bite, consisted of taking a "hair of the dog that bit you" and placing it in the wound.

Halcyon Days. *How did "halcyon days" come to mean a peaceful and pleasurable period of time?*

The original "halcyon days" were fifteen days in the Spring—the seven days preceding the Vernal Equinox in March, the day itself, and the seven days following it. This is the brooding time of the "halcyon" or kingfisher and since its nest was supposed to float on the sea, the superstition arose that calm weather always prevailed at this time of the year.

Half-Cocked. *Where does the expression "go off half-cocked" come from?*

From hunting. A gun at half cock is in the safety position; it cannot be fired. But a hunter may, in his excitement at sighting game, raise the gun to his shoulder and pull the trigger while still "half-cocked." Nothing hap-

114

pens. And so, "to go off half-cocked" means to attempt something in a hurry without proper preparation and to fail in achieving the end.

Half-Seas Over. *Why do we say an intoxicated person is "half-seas over"?*

It's a nautical phrase and originated with the thought that a ship that is halfway across the sea will keep on going rather than turn back. But the application of the expression to an intoxicated person was strengthened by a pun—for the English imported from Holland a strong beer which the Dutch called *op-zee-zober*, meaning "oversea beer."

Halloween. *How did "Halloween" come to be so called?*

The old Celtic calendar began on November 1st and, therefore, October 31st was New Year's Eve—the night on which witches and hobgoblins rode about for one last fling. With the introduction of Christianity the old New Year's Day became "All Saints' Day"; and the evening before became "All Saints' Eve" or "All Hallows' E'en." Though the name was changed, the customs—and the belief that witches rode on this night—persisted and have come down to this day.

Ham Actor. *Why is a poor actor called a "ham"?*

This theatrical slang term contemptuously applied to low-grade actors is a shortening of the term "hamfatter." "Hamfatter" comes from the old-time blackface comedian's practice of putting "ham fat" on his face—so that it would be easy for him to remove the burnt cork after the show. All "whiteface" actors once looked down on "blackface" comedians; many still do.

Hammer and Tongs. *How did we come to use the phrase "hammer and tongs" to mean "energetically"?*

The allusion is to the vim and vigor exhibited by a blacksmith showering blows with his "hammer" upon the iron taken from the forge fire with his "tongs."

Handicap. *Where does the word "handicap" come from?*

The word comes from the usual procedure in drawing lots. Slips of paper are placed in a hat or "cap" and each person in turn draws one out by placing his "hand i' the cap." This practice is still followed in drawing for position in a horse race. Slips bearing the names of the horses are drawn from a hat and the first horse drawn gets the position next the rail, the second horse gets the next position, and so on.

Handkerchief. *What is the origin of the word "handkerchief"?*

The "ker" of this word comes from the Old French *covrir*, meaning "to cover." The "chief" comes from *chef*, meaning "head." A "kerchief" was originally a "head covering," especially the bit of cloth used by women to cover their heads when entering a Catholic Church. A "handkerchief" was one carried in the hand.

Handwriting on the Wall. *Where do we get the expression "handwriting on the wall"?*

It's an allusion to the Bible. According to Daniel 5 "handwriting" appeared on the wall of Belshazzar's palace wall—"Mene, Mene, Tekel, Upharsin." This writing announced to Belshazzar the loss of his kingdom.

116

Hang Fire. *What is the reason a delayed action is said to "hang fire"?*

It's because a flintlock gun does not always go off immediately. Though the spark has been set, the powder in the pan may fizz for a while before exploding the charge behind the shot.

Hangout. *How did "hangout" come to mean a gathering place?*

"Hangout" originally meant a place of business—for at one time almost all professional men, artisans, and tradespeople hung out signs to indicate their occupation and place of business. The term had its origin in the phrase, "Where do you hang out your sign?"

Hannah's Cook. *Where did we get the saying "not worth Hannah's cook"?*

The expression comes down to us from sailing ship days and is a corruption of the phrase "hand or cook." It referred to a whale or fish not worth going after—one for which the captain felt it was not worth risking the life of a single "hand," or even a "cook."

Happy as a Clam. *Why do we use the expression "happy as a clam at high tide" to mean extreme happiness?*

Because clams appear to desire nothing more than to be left alone. Since clams are gathered only when the tide is out, they should be very happy at high tide.

Hard Up. *What is the origin of the slang expression "hard up"?*

It was originally a nautical term. To put the helm "hard up" is to put it as far as possible to windward—in order to turn the ship's head away from the wind. So today, one who has very little money and cannot face a financial storm but must turn away is said to be "hard up."

Harp on Things. *How did the term "harping" come to mean the reiteration of a single point?*

To "harp" is really to play the harp; and the allusion is to an old saying, "Harping on just one string"—in other words, playing the same note over and over again.

Harrier. *Where did cross-country runners get the name "harriers"?*

A dog that is used to chase hares is called a "harrier"—and the first cross-country runs by men were made in playing the game "Hare and Hound."

Harum-Scarum. *What is the origin of the term "harum-scarum"?*

Hare is an old English verb meaning "to excite" or "to worry"—we use it in "harass." The term "harum-scarum" originally meant to "scare 'em" and to "worry 'em."

Haul Over the Coals. *Why do we call a thorough questioning or reprimand being "hauled over the coals"?*

Because at one time those suspected of heresy were literally "hauled over the coals" of a fire in order to induce them to confess their sins and adopt the true faith.

Haywire. *How did the word "haywire" come to be used to describe something that's all in a mess?*

The term seems to have first become popular in the logging camps of the North Woods. In distant camps the teamsters would save the wire from the bales of hay to mend a broken hame-strap or to put a link in a broken chain. Cooks would string haywire above the stove to dry clothes and hang ladles up—and often to bind the stove together. In time, a camp that was notoriously poor in its equipment came to be known as a "haywire" camp; from this usage the term has come to mean "broken," "sick," "crazy" and a score of other things, none of them praiseworthy. The term now commonly means "mixed up"—like a pile of haywire after it's been removed from the bales.

Hearse. *What is the origin of the word "hearse"?*

The word literally means a "harrow"—the Old French for "harrow" being *herse.* The harrows of that time were triangular—and a triangular frame was used to hold the candles set at the head of the coffin. Even today triangular frames are used to hold the candles burning before the statue of a saint in a Catholic Church. Because this candle rack was shaped like a harrow, it too was called a *herse.* Then, since the frame used to carry the coffin from the house to the Church had candles on it, this frame, in turn, was named a *herse.* When carriages were substituted for the frame used to carry a coffin they took the same name—"hearse."

Heart on One's Sleeve. *Where do we get the expression "wearing one's heart on one's sleeve"?*

From chivalry. It was the custom among the knights of old to tie a kerchief, scarf, or other favor from a lady on the sleeve. Since this indicated the state of the man's heart he was said to wear his "heart" on his sleeve.

Heater Piece. *Why is a triangle of land called a "heater piece"?*

Because it looks like a flatiron or "heater." For the same reason, the building erected on the "heater piece" at Fifth Avenue and Twenty-third Street in New York City was called the "Flatiron Building."

Heeled. *What is the reason a person who is well-prepared or in funds is said to be "well-heeled"?*

The term comes to us from the cockpit. A fighting cock has steel gaffs attached to its leg in place of its own spurs. A "well-heeled" bird is one whose fighting gaffs are efficient and effective.

Hell for Leather. *How did we come to use the expression "hell for leather" to describe a fast, reckless horseback ride?*

The original phrase, "all of a lather," didn't seem strong enough—though it does make a little more sense—and so this intensification of it was devised to give the expression a greater feeling of recklessness.

Hep. *Where did "hep" get the meaning "well-informed and up-to-date"?*

In the Army. An Army drill sergeant, in counting the cadence for his marching men, will call out "Hep! Hep!" —a shortening of the words "Step! Step!" The rookie who has learned to "keep in step" (both literally and figuratively) with his companions is "hep." From this we get the present meaning of "one who knows his way around."

Hermetically Sealed. *Why do we say that something that is airtight is "hermetically sealed"?*

Chemists were the first to use an airtight seal. In order to keep air out of a bottle they heated the neck of the bottle until it was soft and then twisted the glass until the opening was sealed. Chemists were once called "Hermes"—after the legendary inventor of chemistry, Hermes Trismegistus—and so "hermetically sealed" means "sealed by the chemists' method."

High Horse. *What is the reason a haughty person is said to be on his "high horse"?*

The horseman has long considered himself superior to those on foot. If the horse is high he's just that much more superior.

High Jinks. *How did we come to call fun and frolic "high jinks"?*

"High Jinks" is a variant of "High Pranks," the name of a once popular game that combined dice and charades—for the fall of the dice determined which member of the group should pretend to be some fictitious character. Of course, playing the game led to fun, frolic and pranks—"high jinks" as we say today.

High-Seas. *What is the origin of the expression "high-seas"?*

By "high-seas" we mean all the waters which are not the property of a particular country—that is, those beyond the three-mile limit. The word "high" is used to indicate that the seas are public, just as "highway" means a "public way." In both cases, of course, "high" also means "chief" or "principal."

Hippopotamus. *Where did the "hippopotamus" get that name?*

The name comes directly from two Greek words—*hippos* and *potamós*—and literally means "river horse."

Hit It Off. *Why do we say two people who get on well together "hit it off"?*

To "hit it off" originally meant to "strike the scent"—as in hunting. So, two people who find they have something in common "hit the scent"—and are off!

Hitch. *What is the reason a temporary setback is called a "hitch" in our plans?*

The "hitch" in our plans is like the "hitch" that develops when a horse is lame. The word comes from the Scottish *hitch*, meaning "motion by jerks." If we set out on horseback and our horse develops a limp, we can't arrive in time and there's a "hitch in our plans."

Hobby. *How did one's avocation come to be called one's "hobby"?*

A plow horse is called "Dobbin," "Robin," or "Hobin." From this latter we get the diminutive "hobby," meaning "a small horse." "Hobby" is used in this sense in referring to a child's toy or "hobby horse." A toy horse just furnishes amusement—it cannot be worked. So an occupation pursued for amusement and not as "work" is a "hobby."

Hobnob. *Why do we say two people in intimate conversation are "hobnobbing" together?*

The term was once spelled "habnab" and its meaning was "have and not have." As a synonym for "give and take" it's an apt description of an intimate conversation.

122

Hobson's Choice. *Where did we get the expression "Hobson's choice"—and its meaning of "no choice at all"?*

From Tobias Hobson, who kept a livery stable in Cambridge, England, in the seventeenth century. Hobson let out his horses only in rotation, saying, "This or none." "Hobson's choice" is "no choice at all."

Hocus-Pocus. *Why do we say "hocus-pocus" when doing a magic trick?*

Because there once was a wizard named Ochus Bochus who did all sorts of tricks; he appears in Scandinavian mythology and "hocus-pocus" is just a corruption of his name.

Hodgepodge. *What is the reason a mixture of a little of this and a little of that is called a "hodgepodge"?*

This is a corruption of the term "hotchpotch" and a "hotchpotch" is a stew made up of a little of this and a little of that—a sort of hash.

Hoe-Cake. *How did the "hoe-cake" get that name?*

It came about because in pioneer homes this Indian corn bread was often baked on the broad thin blade of the hoe used in the cotton fields.

Hold a Candle. *What is the reason we say that an inferior person "cannot hold a candle" to a superior one?*

In the Roman Catholic Church a candle is held or placed before the image of a favorite Saint in praying to that Saint for a special favor. A person who "cannot hold a candle" to another—that is, who cannot even pray to him —is indeed inferior.

123

Honeymoon. *Why do we call the period that immediately follows a marriage a "honeymoon"?*

The "honey" alludes to the sweetness of marriage delights; the "moon" to the rapidity with which they wane.

Hooch. *Where did we get the word "hooch" as a synonym for strong drink?*

From Alaska. When America acquired Alaska in 1867, a small body of troops was sent into the territory. Since the soldiers were forbidden to bring any alcoholic beverages along with them, they set up their own stills and brewed a very powerful drink from sugar and flour. The Alaskan natives called this drink *hoochinoo*—the name by which it was known until the gold rush to the Klondike; then *hoochinoo* was shortened to "hooch."

Hoodlum. *How did a ruffian come to be called a "hoodlum"?*

It's all due to illegible handwriting. In an attempt to coin a name for a San Francisco gang, a reporter took the name of the gang-leader, Muldoon, and reversed it—making it "Noodlum." The typesetter couldn't read his writing and set it up as "Hoodlum."

Hook and Ladder. *Why is the fire truck that carries the ladders to the fire called a "hook and ladder"?*

Because in times past—and even today—a ladder with a hook on the end of it was used by firemen in scaling a building. This hook on the end of the ladder gave the name to the fire apparatus.

Hook or Crook. *What is the reason we use the expression "by hook or crook" to mean "by fair means or foul"?*

This expression contains a double pun. Both "hook" and "crook" mean a shepherd's "crook"; both also mean a thief's "hook." The allusion, therefore, to "fair means or foul" is doubly accented.

Hoosegow. *How did a jail get the name "hoosegow"?*

The term comes from the Spanish word for "judged" or "sentenced"—*juzgado*. This is pronounced by Mexican peons as though there were no "d" in the word—almost exactly like "hoosegow." Since a peon seldom had enough money to pay his fine, to be sentenced meant to be sent to jail. Because of this, a Mexican would explain his absence from an American's ranch by saying *juzgado*. The American, knowing the peon had been in jail, assumed the term meant "jail"—and so came to call a "jail" a "hoosegow."

Hoot. *Why do we use the expression "I don't give a hoot" to show our unconcern?*

A "hoot" is, of course, a shout of derision and contempt. A person so unconcerned that he doesn't even care to "give a hoot" in derision is, presumably, totally uninterested.

Hopping Mad. *How did the phrase "hopping mad" come to stand for extreme anger?*

Because if you're angry enough, you will use not only your tongue and your hands to express your emotion but also your feet—and then you'll be "hopping mad."

Hopscotch. *Does the "scotch" in the name of the game "hopscotch" refer to its Scottish origin?*

No. The "scotch" just means "scratch." In playing the game you must "hop" over the lines "scratched" in the ground.

Hornbook. *What is the reason the "hornbook" was given that name?*

The early primers of England were made of a thin board on which were printed the alphabet, the digits, and the "Lord's Prayer." This was covered with a thin sheet of horn in order to keep it from becoming soiled.

Horse Latitudes. *How did the "horse latitudes" get that name?*

The region of calms between 30 degrees and 35 degrees North latitude got the name "horse latitudes" because ships laden with horses and cattle for America and the West Indies were often becalmed there for so long that the horses died.

Horse Radish. *Why is the "horse radish" so called?*

"Horse" is often used to mean "coarse"—as in "horse mackerel" and "horse bean." The "horse radish" looks something like the common radish but is far more coarse in texture—and stronger in flavor.

Horse Sense. *What is the "sense" referred to in the expression "horse sense"?*

The allusion is not to the sense of a horse—it hasn't too much—but to the shrewdness of horse traders.

126

How Do You Do? *Why do we use the phrase "how do you do" as a greeting?*

The last "do" means "fare" and we're really asking, "How are things going?"

Hubba-Hubba. *How did "hubba-hubba" come to be chosen as the modern "wolf call"?*

In much the same way as the word "barbarian" came to be adopted. The ancient Greeks felt that foreigners spoke in nonsense syllables—foreign languages sounded like a series of "ba-ba" sounds to them—and so they called foreigners "barbarians." In like manner, the American soldier in the Pacific during World War II considered the native languages, as far as he was concerned, just so much "hubbub." Basing his choice on this word, he picked two nonsense syllables of his own to use in calling out upon seeing a native girl—"hubba-hubba."

Humble Pie. *Why do we say an apologetic person "eats humble pie"?*

Because of a pun. The entrails of deer are called "umbles" and at one time these "umbles" were made into a pie which the servants and huntsmen of a lord ate —while the lord and his guests ate the carcass. So a person who humbled himself was said to "eat humble pie."

Hunky-Dory. *Where did we get the expression "everything is hunky-dory"?*

From the Low Dutch word *honk*, meaning "safe." The word was also used to mean a "goal" in a game—and so a man who scored or who safely reached base in a game like baseball was said to "honk" or "be honky." "Dory," quite possibly, comes from "all right."

127

Hurrah. *Who were the first people to shout "hurrah"?*

The Prussians first used this word as a battle cry in the War of Liberation of 1812. The German interjection, *hurrâ* comes from *huren,* meaning "to rush." But many other nations use similar words as a battle cry.

Hussy. *Why is an unpleasant or immoral woman called a "hussy"?*

The word is just a corruption of "housewife" and originally had no unkind implications attached to it, although for many years it was not applied to a married woman.

QUIZ 4

(Answers on page 272)

1. Why do we say a person with spunk has "grit"?
2. What is the origin of the term "goodbye"?
3. How did a tailor's pressing iron come to be called a "goose"?
4. Why do we say a person who talks well has the gift of "gab"?
5. Where did we get the name "guerrilla" for an irregular soldier?
6. How did the "harmonica" come to be called that?
7. Why do we say a person who is a success "makes a hit"?
8. What is the origin of the term "hydrophobia"?
9. How did a robbery come to be called a "holdup"?
10. Why do we call unnecessary praise "gilding the lily"?
11. What is the reason a person who is working hard is said to "hump himself"?
12. How did we come to call an old man a "gaffer"?
13. Why is a lively person said to be full of "ginger"?
14. What is the origin of the expression, "that's a horse of another color"?
15. Where did illegal whiskey get the name "moonshine"?
16. Why is a "greengrocer" called that?
17. What is the origin of the expression "Dutch rub"?
18. How did prison come to be called the "clink"?
19. Why do we use the term "horsefeathers" to mean "nonsense"?
20. What is the reason we call a minor annoyance a "mere flea bite"?

```
I I I I I I I I I
I                 I
I        I        I
I                 I
I I I I I I I I I
```

Idiot. *Has the word "idiot" always meant a mentally de-ficient person?*

No. The word is Greek and at first an "idiot" was just a private citizen who held no public office. However, since the Greeks considered it a great honor to hold office, the word finally came to mean a person who couldn't take part in public affairs.

In at the Death. *What is the origin of the term "in at the death"?*

In fox hunting it's considered very desirable to keep up with the dogs—or at least to have arrived by the time the treed fox is killed. Every fox hunter tries to be "in at the death."

In the Groove. *Why do we say in approval of a musician's improvisations, "He's in the groove"?*

The allusion is to the phonograph record and needle. When the needle is "in the groove" the music sounds fine; when it is out of the groove it's terrible.

In the Same Boat. *How did "all in the same boat" come to mean equality of opportunity—or lack of it?*

The allusion is to a shipwreck. When a ship is wrecked and has to be abandoned, all distinction of class must be abandoned as well. Each man must accept and share the common fate—they're "all in the same boat."

In the Swim. *Where do we get the expression "in the swim"?*

From fishing. Anglers call a gathering of fish a "swim." The term was eventually applied to social gatherings at which people came together in large groups. And so, to be "in the swim" is to be a part of such gatherings.

Inaugurate. *What is the reason we say we "inaugurate" a man when he is installed in office?*

The term is from the Latin *inaugurare* which means "to take omens from the flight of birds." No Roman official was installed without the approval of the birds.

India Rubber. *Where did "India rubber" get this name?*

The same mistake that led Columbus to think he had reached India when he discovered America led to people's calling rubber "India rubber." Columbus reported that on his second voyage he found the natives of Haiti playing a game with "balls made from the gum of a tree."

Indian Giver. *Why is a person who gives someone a gift and then expects to receive something in return called an "Indian giver"?*

At one time Indians were not well thought of and their customs were not well understood. The Indian who expected the white man to follow Indian custom and make a return gift was considered to be more interested in gain than in being generous.

Indian Summer. *How did a warm spell in late fall get the name "Indian summer"?*

Since the term "Indian" was once used generally to indicate something "sham" or "bogus," the sham summer of late fall came to be called "Indian summer."

Infantry. *What is the origin of the word "infantry"?*

The term comes from the word "infant"—since this part of the army was originally made up of the page boys of the knights.

Inside Track. *Where did we get the expression "he's got the inside track"?*

From horse racing. The best position for a horse, the shortest to the ultimate goal, is the one nearest the rail—the "inside track."

Irish Luck. *Why do we call a surprising turn of good luck the "luck of the Irish"?*

Because the Irish were always poor but managed to pull through somehow. The potato crop failed but they didn't all die of hunger; the "Big Wind" blew all night but then it went out to sea again; the "luck of the Irish" pulled them through.

Irons in the Fire. *What is the origin of the expression "too many irons in the fire"?*

The allusion is to the blacksmith who generally keeps several pieces of iron in the fire—in order to always have one ready for his anvil. But if he has too many in the fire at the same time he can't watch them all and attend to them all when they need attention.

132

```
J J J J J J J J
J               J
J    J          J
J               J
J J J J J J J J
```

Jack Robinson. *What is the origin of the expression "before you can say Jack Robinson"?*

There are several explanations of this phrase; but the best story is of a very volatile gentleman-about-town named Jack Robinson. Robinson used to go calling on his friends and would then change his mind and leave before his name could be announced.

Jalopy. *How did the "jalopy" get that name?*

An old and dilapidated automobile rides more like a horse than a smooth-running modern car; the motion is "gallop-y" and from this we get, by a softening of the sound of the *g*, "jalopy."

Jam Session. *Why is a gathering of musicians during which they play together without scores called a "jam session"?*

It's because the musicians—who are playing for their own amusement—"jam" or crowd as many notes as possible into a bar of music, as each in turn improvises.

Jazz. *Where does the word "jazz" come from?*

The word comes to us from Creole French—by way of the minstrel show dandy who carried a cane and wore spats, "Mr. Jasbo." In Creole French a "dandy" is called a *chasse beaux*—or a "beaux chaser"—because he's so attractive that he chases all the other beaux away. The syncopated music we now call "jazz" was used in the "cakewalk"—a form of competition for these "beaux" at box socials. Minstrel shows adopted the character, the dance, the music, the name of the dance and the name *chasse beaux* for the competitors—but, not knowing French, spelled the latter, "Jassbo," "Jasbo" and "Jazz-bo." The vulgar meaning of the term has its origin in another characteristic of the original *beaux*.

Jeep. *Why is a "jeep" called that?*

The first quarter-ton reconnaissance cars delivered to the Army had painted on their sides the letters "G.P."—which stood for "General Purpose." "G.P." when said quickly became "jeep." The utterance of a character in the "Popeye" comic strip of Elzie Crisler Segar, "Eugene the Jeep"—who confines himself to saying, "Jeep, jeep, jeep"—may have helped popularize the word.

Jerkwater Town. *What is the reason a small town is called a "jerkwater town"?*

On a long trip a railroad train will have to stop now and again to get water for the engine from an overhead water tower. These towers are equipped with long nozzles that are pulled down over the tender. When a train gets water in this manner, it is said to "jerk water." If a town is so small and unimportant that the only reason the train stops there is to get water, it's called a "jerkwater town."

134

Jerry-Built. *How did a poorly built house come to be called "jerry-built"?*

"Jerry" comes from "jury" and "jury" from the Old French word *ajurie*, meaning "relief." The term is similar to the nautical "jury mast" or "jury rig"—a temporary mast or rigging set up when a ship's regular mast and rigging have been carried away by a storm. Hence a "jerry-built" house is one that's not built to last.

Jerusalem Artichoke. *Has the "Jerusalem artichoke" any connection with the city of Jerusalem?*

Only through an error. "Jerusalem artichokes" are members of the sunflower family, and the Italian word for "sunflower" is *girasole*. The artichoke's name is just a corruption of this word.

Jiminy, Jingo, Gee. *What is the origin of the expletive "by Jiminy, Jingo, Gee"?*

"By Jiminy" is a scholarly euphemism for "by the gods." "Jiminy" refers to the Gemini—the Heavenly Twins of the Zodiac and the patron gods of ancient Rome. "Jingo" comes to us from the Basque language; the Basque name for "God" is *Jinko*. "Gee" stands for the "G" of "God."

Jitterbug. *Where did the "jitterbug" get his name?*

From the bugs themselves—those little bugs you see scooting about on the surface of still ponds in the spring. The appropriateness of the term is reinforced by the meaning of "jitter"—"to act in a nervous manner"—and the fact that "bug" is a name for an enthusiast, and also for a crazy person.

135

Jive. *Why are "jive" music and dancing called that?*

To "duck and dive" is a term applied to square dancing —one of the calls being: "Duck for the oyster; dive for the clam." Similarly, and in apposition to this, modern athletic dancers "jump and"—for alliteration and rhyme —"jive."

Joe Miller. *How did an old and stale joke come to be called a "Joe Miller"?*

Joe Miller was an actor who lived from 1684 to 1738 and attained quite a reputation as a humorist. In the early eighteenth century John Mottley made a collection of jokes and credited them to Joe Miller in a book called "Joe Miller's Jests." This is the standard source book for old jokes— and so any old joke is called a "Joe Miller."

Jog the Memory. *What is the reason we say we "jog the memory"?*

"Jog" really means "shake" and when we "jog a person's memory" we shake it up. Likewise a "jog trot" is a shaking trot.

John of Bohemia. *Where did the expression "he fights like King John of Bohemia" come from, and why does it mean "fighting blind"?*

King John of Bohemia was an ally of Philip of France at the Battle of Crecy on August 26, 1346, in which the French suffered overwhelming defeat by the English. King John was completely blind but insisted upon being guided into the thick of the battle—where he died fighting his unseen foes.

John Bull. *Why is the name "John Bull" used to represent England?*

The "Bull" is an allusion to the British fondness for beef —just as a Dutchman is called "John Cheese." But a Scottish satirist, Dr. John Arbuthnot, published in 1712 a pamphlet that popularized the term. It was entitled "The History of John Bull" and in it Dr. Arbuthnot named his characters after animals. He called the Frenchman "Lewis Baboon," the Dutchman "Nicholas Frog," and the Englishman "John Bull."

Johnny-Cake. *How did "johnny-cakes" get their name?*

The Shawnee Indians of the Cumberland Mountain region made a cake of maize and baked it upon a flat stone which had been previously heated in the fire. Trappers adopted the custom from the Indians and called them "Shawnee-cakes." Later settlers who adopted the cakes failed to understand the meaning of their name and so changed it to "johnny-cakes."

Joint. *Why do we call a "dive" a "joint"?*

Because it's a place where people congregate. "Joint" comes from the Latin *junctus*, meaning "joined."

Jordan Almond. *Has the name "Jordan almond" anything to do with the river Jordan?*

Not a thing. The name comes from the Middle English *jardyne almaunde*, meaning a "cultivated almond"—as opposed to a "wild" one.

Josh. *What is the origin of the word "josh"?*

The Scottish have a word *joss*, meaning "to jostle" or "push against." This word—influenced by the name of

137

the American humorous writer, Josh Billings—gave us the present word and its meaning: "to push around humorously."

Jot. *Why do we say "not a jot" and "I don't care a jot"?*

The "jot" here referred to is the Greek letter "iota"—which was often written merely as a dot below a long vowel. When written thus, it was the smallest of all Greek letters.

Jubilee. *Where does the word "jubilee" come from?*

From the Hebrew *yōbēl*, meaning "ram's horn." According to the Book of Leviticus in the Bible, fifty years after the Jews were freed from Egyptian bondage they were to declare a year of rest in which the fields were to lie fallow and all Hebrew slaves were to be freed. The start of the Jewish year is announced by blowing a ram's horn on Rosh Hashana.

Jug. *How did a jail come to be called a "jug"?*

Originally a "jug" was not a prison but a pillory. The word comes from the French *joug*, meaning "yoke." When the pillory was abolished and the prisoners were transferred to jail the name "jug" was transferred with them.

Juggernaut. *What is the reason tanks, trucks and other large vehicles are called "juggernauts"?*

The god, Vishnu, one of the Hindu Trinity, has a thousand names. One of these is *Jagannatha*, meaning "Lord of the World." In Hindu mythology this god owns a car which is forty-five feet high and has sixteen wheels, each of which is seven feet in diameter. And so, any big vehicle on wheels is called for him a "juggernaut."

138

Juke Box. *Where did the "juke box" get that name?*

The more ecstatic religious revival meetings in the South produce a sort of frenzy characterized by rhythmic "jumps" and "jerks." When in such a state a person is said to "juke"—from a combination of the two words. Dancers, under the stimulation of extremely "hot" music, will likewise "juke"; music that produces this state is "juke music"—and so, since the coin machine phonograph specializes in this type of music, it's a "juke box."

Jump Over the Broomstick. *What is the origin of the expression "she jumped over the broomstick"?*

A woman who started living with a man without any marriage ceremony generally ignored housewifely duties—pots, pans, and the broomstick. So, she was said to "jump over the broom," or "broomstick." It's interesting to note that the phrase sired a custom. Women entering into such a relationship would, instead of allowing themselves to be carried over the threshold of their new home, jump over a broomstick into it.

Junket. *Why is the dessert, "junket" called that?*

The Italians called bulrushes *giunco*. They served a cream or curd cheese on a mat made of these leaves—and so called the cheese *giuncata*. From this the English derived the word "junket"—which first meant a curded cream cheese served with spices.

```
K K K K K K
K           K
K    K      K
K           K
K K K K K K
```

Kangaroo. *How did the "kangaroo" get its name?*

Captain James Cook, who discovered Australia, asked the tribesmen of the Endeavor River region the name of the animal. They answered, "Kangaroo." Whether that was the name of the animal itself or just an answer signifying "I don't know" is something that we don't know.

Kangaroo Court. *Why is a mock trial held by convicts called a "kangaroo court"?*

The term originated in Australia at the time when it was a penal colony and the use of "kangaroo" is an allusion to the prisoners' belief that they had no more to say about what happened to them than the kangaroos of that continent.

Keelhaul. *What is the reason a severe reprimand is called "a keelhauling"?*

In certain European navies it was once the practice to tie a delinquent sailor to a yardarm, attach a weight to his feet, and then by means of a rope "haul" him from one side of the ship to the other beneath the "keel." The result was often fatal.

Kettle of Fish. *How did we come to call a muddled situation a "pretty kettle of fish"?*

A very popular Scottish picnic is called a "kettle of fish" —from the fact that the picnickers catch salmon or trout in the streams of the countryside and cook them in a large "kettle" for the main course of the picnic meal. We have a similar phrase—"pretty picnic"—with a similar meaning. Since "picnics" are seldom "pretty" and often do not operate smoothly, these terms both mean the opposite of what they say.

Kibitzer. *Where did the "kibitzer" get that name?*

The term comes, via Yiddish, from the German *kiebitz* —meaning a peewit or lapwing—and the allusion is to such a bird's sitting on one's shoulder while one plays cards. "The note of the peewit," says John Burroughs, "is a human sigh and the bird's two-syllable call frequently conveys that idea. Often the bird seems to be saying, 'Dear me,' in a tone which is plaintive and resigned rather than petulant and impatient."

Kick Up a Row. *How did we come to use "kick" as a synonym for "start" in the expression "kick up a row"?*

Because it is a schoolboy's way of starting a fight. The boy kicks dirt onto his proposed opponent.

Kid. *What is the reason we call a child a "kid"?*

The Anglo-Saxon word for "child" is *cild*. In ancient times—just as today—folks often failed to pronounce the letter "l." The similarity of sound between this name for a child and that for a young goat, and the similarity of antics, led to the use of "kid" as a synonym for "child."

141

Kilkenny Cats. *Why do we say two bitter opponents "fight like Kilkenny cats"?*

Because of the Irish legend of two cats that fought until only their tails remained. This legend is supposed to refer to an equally destructive contest between the towns of Kilkenny and Irishtown.

Killed by Inches. *How did we come to adopt the phrase "killed by inches"?*

The allusion is to the various ways of prolonging death by torture. Procrustes' bed stretched men to death; the iron coffin of Lissa had a lid which was lowered slowly but surely down inside the coffin until ultimately it crushed its victim.

Killed by Kindness. *Where did we get the expression "killed by kindness"?*

From the story of Draco, the Athenian legislator, who died because of his popularity. The Greeks used to wave their caps and cloaks as a sign of approval and when they were extremely enthusiastic they tossed their hats and their clothing at the object of their enthusiasm. In the sixth century B.C., Draco aroused the enthusiasm of the audience in the theatre of Aegina to such an extent that the entire gathering showered him with caps and cloaks—and smothered him to death.

Kindergarten. *How did the "kindergarten" get that name?*

"Kindergarten" is a German word that literally means "children's garden." The term was originated by Friedrich Froebel, the German educator, who introduced the

142

idea that a school for young children should gratify and cultivate the child's normal aptitude for exercise, play, imitation, and construction—just as playing in a garden would do.

Kit and Caboodle. *What is the origin of the expression "whole kit and caboodle"?*

The Dutch word *boedel* means "effects"—what a person owns. Robbers, especially housebreakers, adopted the term—calling whatever they stole "boodle." They carried their burglar's tools in a "kit." If they were able to enter a house, gather up everything valuable, and make a clean escape, they said they had gotten away with "kit and boodle." In time, the phrase was shortened to "caboodle"—the "ca" standing for the "kit." Then the "kit" was reintroduced into the phrase—probably for emphasis.

Kite Checks. *Why do we say a person who gives a check on an insufficient bank account is "kiting" the check?*

The term alludes to kiteflying—for if you fly a kite, you can never tell definitely when it is coming down to earth. So too, if you "kite a check" you're never quite certain it won't be presented for collection before you have sufficient money to cover it in the bank. The practice originated as an exchange of checks between two banks or business firms. Each gave the other a check; each deposited the other's check in his bank account—and so for a short while each apparently had a larger balance than was actually the case. For many years this was considered a perfectly ethical business practice among banks, business firms, and well-established individuals.

143

Kitty. *How did the common pool of a poker game come to be called the "kitty"?*

The term comes from the Middle English word *kist*—from which we also get our modern word "chest." A *kist* was a "money box"—and so, quite logically, the word was applied to the pool in a poker game. From being called the "kist," it became the "kit," and finally the "kitty."

Knickers. *Why are knee-length golfing trousers called "knickers"?*

In Dutch, *knickerbacker* is the name of a man who bakes clay marbles. Washington Irving chose a variant of this name, "Knickerbocker," as his pseudonym when writing his "History of New York." Cruikshank's illustrations for this book showed the citizens of old New York wearing loose pantaloons caught in at the knee—and so the garments were called "knickerbockers" or "knickers."

Know the Ropes. *Where do we get the expression "know the ropes"?*

From sailing. The original allusion was to an experienced sailor—who "knew the ropes" aboard ship. But the current allusion is to the ropes or "wires" used by a "wirepuller."

Knuckle Under. *What is the reason we say a man who gives in "knuckles under"?*

Originally, a "knuckle" was any joint—we still occasionally say "knuckle of veal"—and in this expression the "knuckle" referred to is the knee. When you "knuckle under" you kneel in submission.

Kowtow. *Where does the word "kowtow" come from?*

The word is Chinese and literally means "knock the head." It was an ancient Chinese custom to touch the ground with the forehead when worshipping or paying one's respects to an illustrious personage.

Kris Kringle. *How did Santa Claus get the name "Kris Kringle"?*

Through an error. We use this term to mean "Santa Claus," the patron saint of Christmas, but it comes from the German name for the "Christ Child"—*Christkindlein*.

QUIZ 5

(Answers on page 274)

1. *Why do we call small change "chicken feed"?*
2. *How did an old worn-out joke come to be called a "wheeze"?*
3. *What is the origin of the term "kidnap"?*
4. *Why is a "jaywalker" known by that name?*
5. *How did a swinging knockout blow come to be called a "haymaker"?*
6. *What is the origin of the expression "quit your kidding"?*
7. *Where does the expression "off the track" come from?*
8. *Why do we say a person who has died has "kicked the bucket"?*
9. *Where did we get the expression "keeled over" to describe someone knocked flat?*
10. *What is the origin of the term "icky"?*
11. *How did baseball "innings" get that name?*
12. *Why is the man who rides the horses in a race called a "jockey"?*
13. *Where did we get the expression "kingdom come"?*
14. *What does the "G" of "G-man" stand for?*
15. *Why is a rapid vehicle said to "burn up the dust"?*
16. *How did a stupid person come to be called a "blockhead"?*
17. *What is the origin of the expression "give her the gun"?*
18. *Why is the actor who plays the villain called a "heavy"?*
19. *What is the reason a person who holds another in close conversation is said to "buttonhole" him?*
20. *Where does the term "scram" come from?*

146

```
L L L L L L L
L           L
L    L      L
L           L
L L L L L L L
```

Lackadaisical. *Why do we say a lazy, dawdling person is "lackadaisical"?*

It's a bit of keen psychological observation. The term comes from the exclamation, "lackaday," which means "shame on you, day"—just as though the "day" were a person. And since most persons who cry "lackaday" and blame the quick passage of time are looking for an excuse for their own lack of energy, they are "lackadaisical."

Laconic. *Where does the word "laconic" come from?*

From "Laconia"—the general name for Spartan territory. The Spartans were noted for their brusque speech—the best example of it being their reply when Philip of Macedon wrote to their magistrates: "If I enter Laconia I will level Lacedaemon to the ground." The Spartans' reply was: "If."

Lager Beer. *How did "lager beer" get that name?*

The German word *lager* means a "storehouse." The barrels of lager beer are placed in a storehouse for their contents to age.

147

Lagniappe. *What is the origin of the term "lagniappe"?*
This name for a trifling gift from a merchant to his customer originated in New Orleans. The Quichuan Indian language has a word *yapa* with the same meaning. In Caribbean countries this is generally *ñapa*. The French of New Orleans, in adopting this term, added the article, *la*.

Lallapaloosa. *Where does the term "lallapaloosa" come from?*
"Lallapaloosa" comes from a provincialism of County Mayo, Ireland—*allay-foozee*, meaning a "sturdy fellow." The Irish adopted it from the French—who, when they landed at Killala in 1798, repeatedly shouted, *Allez-fusil!* —meaning, "Forward the muskets."

Lame Duck. *Why is a member of Congress who has failed to be reelected called a "lame duck"?*
Wild ducks in flight fly together—their heads outstretched in front, their legs outstretched behind. A "lame duck" can't keep up with the flock. So too, a member of the British Stock Exchange who couldn't meet his liabilities on settling day couldn't keep up with the flock and was struck off the list. From this we get our use of the term in reference to members of Congress who fail to be reelected and can't continue in office.

Landlubber. *How did the "landlubber" get that name?*
The "lubber" is not, as so many suppose, from "lover," but from the Danish *lobbes*, meaning a "clown" or "bumpkin." So the term means any person who lives on land and acts inexperienced or awkward aboard a ship.

148

Larboard. *What is the origin of the term "larboard"?*

"Larboard" is from the Old English *lade-bord*—meaning "loading side." Since the steering oar of early sailing vessels was on the starboard side, the opposite side was brought up to the docks for loading.

Larceny. *Where did the word "larceny" get the meaning "theft"?*

In France—where mercenary troops were generally expected to indulge in petty theft. The French word for a mercenary soldier is *larcin*.

Lavender. *Why was the flower known as "lavender" given that name?*

It was once the custom—now, unfortunately, no longer followed—for laundresses to place a sprig of this plant in with the laundry they had cleaned in order to scent it. The Italian word for washing is *lavanda*.

Lay an Egg. *How did the expression "lay an egg" become associated with a joke that falls flat?*

A hen that lays an egg makes a great fuss over it but the other hens pay little or no attention to her. When a comedian tells a joke and makes a great fuss about it but no one else does, then he too is said to have "laid an egg."

Leap Year. *Why is "leap year" so called?*

Normally, as one year follows another, the day of the month which falls on a Monday this year will fall on a Tuesday next year, and on a Wednesday the following year. In the fourth year it will—after February—"leap over" Thursday and fall on a Friday.

Learn by Heart. *How does it happen we say we learn things "by heart" instead of "by head"?*

It's because of a mistaken analysis of anatomical functions made by the ancient Greeks. They placed the seat of thought in the heart.

Learn by Rote. *What is the reason we use the phrase "learn by rote" to indicate learning by repetition?*

This phrase means "to learn by the wheel"—from *rota*, the Latin word for "wheel." The allusion is to turning the thought over and over in the mind or saying it over and over again, in much the same way as a wheel goes around.

Leatherneck. *Where did the United States Marines get their nickname "leatherneck"?*

Sailors gave them that name—from the fact that in 1805 a stout leather collar was sewed on the Marines' coats to ward off enemy sword strokes.

Legend. *Why do we call a fable a "legend"?*

The word comes from the Latin *legenda*, which in turn comes from *legere*, meaning "to read." The original "Legenda" was a book containing the lives of the saints read at convents and monasteries, but it included so much that was far-fetched and miraculous that the word "legend" got its current meaning.

Leopard. *How did the "leopard" get its name?*

Because of a mistake. It was once wrongly believed that the leopard was a cross between a "leo" (that is, a lion) and a "pard" (that is, a white panther)—hence the name "leopard."

Let George Do It. *Who is the "George" of the expression "let George do it"?*

This expression is believed to have originated in France in the fifteenth century in a satirical reference—*laissez faire à Georges*—to the many activities of Cardinal Georges d'Amboise, Archbishop of Rouen and Prime Minister of Louis XII.

Let Her Rip. *Why do we use the expression "let her rip" to mean let everything go as it will?*

The "rip" is a callous punning on "R.I.P."—*requiescat in pace*—the Latin inscription placed on graves. This phrase means "rest in peace." When we "let her rip" we let "her" do just the opposite.

Lewd. *How did the word "lewd" acquire its present meaning?*

This is an old Anglo-Saxon word *loewed*, meaning "lay" —as opposed to the clergy. Thus it originally meant "people generally." But since at one time only the clergy were able to read or write, "lewd" was used to mean "the unlearned." From "unlearned" it came to mean "base"—and, ultimately, "vulgar language and behavior" —especially in a sexual sense.

Lick into Shape. *What is the origin of the expression "to lick into shape"?*

It was once believed that bear cubs were shapeless at birth and that they remained that way until the mother bear awoke from her long winter's nap and literally "licked them into shape."

151

Lieutenant. *Why does a "lieutenant" general outrank a "major" general?*

Because a "lieutenant" was originally a substitute. The word comes from the Latin phrase *locum tenens*, meaning "holding the place"—of another, that is—and because of this meaning a lieutenant general should be second only to a full general in rank: he is.

Life of Reilly. *Where did we get the expression, "living the life of Reilly"?*

This expression had its origin in a comic song of the 1880's about a saloonkeeper in a small town in the Middle West who prospered so much that he was able to raise his saloon to the dignity of a hotel. The song was called "Is That Mr. Reilly?" and was sung by the original Pat Rooney. The chorus goes:

"Is that Mister Reilly, can any one tell?
Is that Mister Reilly who owns the hotel?
Well, if that's Mister Reilly they speak of so highly,
Upon my soul, Reilly, you're doing quite well."

Lily-Livered. *Why do we say a coward is "lily-livered"?*

Because the ancient Greeks believed that the liver was the seat of passion. Dark bile indicated strong passion; light bile, weakness. The person whose bile was lily-colored or white just had no "guts" at all.

Limbo. *What is the origin of the term "limbo"?*

In school theology many an infant who has died cannot go to Heaven—because he hasn't been baptized. But neither can he go to Hell—because he hasn't sinned. The child must therefore stand on the dividing line between the two—and the Latin word *limbus* means "the edge."

Limelight. *Why do we say that a person of prominence is "in the limelight"?*

Because at one time, calcium—or "lime"—was a necessary element in making the light of a spotlight. In order to produce a brilliant white light a stream of oxygen and one of hydrogen were burned upon a ball of lime.

Limey. *How did the British sailor get the nickname "limey"?*

This name for a sailor in the British Navy goes back to 1795—when lime juice was issued by the Admiralty as an anti-scorbutic. The sailor was first called a "lime-juicer" and then a "limey."

Lion's Share. *What is the reason the major portion of something is called the "lion's share"?*

The allusion is to one of Aesop's fables—in which the "lion's share" is all. In this fable the lion went hunting with the fox and the ass. As they were about to divide the game, the lion spoke up and demanded one third as the share agreed upon and one third by virtue of his sovereignty. "And as for the remaining portion," said the lion, "I defy anyone to take it from me."

Lit. *Why is an intoxicated person said to be "lit"?*

It so happens that those who drink quantities of liquor generally end up with a red nose. This, in slang, is a "lantern" or "lighthouse." It's quite obvious that such a "lantern" is "lit" by imbibing more liquor.

Lobbying. *Where did we get the expression "lobbying"?*

Men who wished to promote special interests were at one time allowed the use of the legislative chambers. Be-

153

cause of their insidious persistence, however, they were ultimately banished to the "lobby" of the chambers—where they seemed to do just about as well.

Lock, Stock and Barrel. *How did "lock, stock and barrel" come to mean "all"?*

There are three parts to a gun—the barrel, the stock, and the firing mechanism, or lock. By enumerating all three the totality is reaffirmed.

Logrolling. *What is the reason legislators who trade off votes are said to be "logrolling"?*

The allusion is to a common practice in lumbering. Men of different lumber camps will agree to join forces and help roll each other's logs—for this is the hardest part of lumbering.

Lollypop. *Why is a "lollypop" so called?*

In the northern part of England the word "lolly" means "tongue." A lump of candy that you "pop" in and out of your mouth onto your tongue is quite aptly called a "lollypop."

Lombard Loan. *Where does the term "Lombard Loan" come from?*

Indirectly, from Italy. "Lombard loans" are those which bear a higher-than-average rate of interest—because the enterprises for which they are made, or the collateral on which they are based, carry a higher-than-average amount of risk. The loans were named after the street where such moneylenders were found—Lombard Street in London. The street was named for the home of the moneylenders—Lombardi, Italy.

154

Long Run. *Why do we use "in the long run" to mean the final outcome?*

The reference is to a race—best illustrated in the story of the hare who was ahead for a while but lost out to the tortoise "in the long run."

Longshoreman. *What is the "long" doing in the word "longshoreman"?*

In the past when ships were unloaded the sailors passed the goods from the ships to men "along" the shore—and so they were called " 'long-shore-men."

Loony. *Is there any relationship to the loon implied in the term "loony"?*

Yes—though the loon is not a crazy bird, his weird, loud cry sounds like the laughter of an insane person. However, the choice of the word was no doubt influenced by its similarity in sound to "lunacy."

Lord of Misrule. *Who is the "Lord of Misrule" supposed to be?*

The term is not a synonym for the devil. The "Lord of Misrule" was originally the "Abbot of Misrule"—the person designated a "Master of Revels," somewhat like the "King" of a Mardi Gras.

Lotus Eater. *Where did the person who fritters away his time get the name "lotus eater"?*

In Homer's "Odyssey"—where those who ate the fruit of the lotus tree forgot their friends and homes and lost all desire to return.

155

Love. *Why do we use the word "love" to mean "nothing" in tennis?*

The term comes from the French *l'oeuf*, meaning "egg." The French use it to designate "no score" or "zero" because an egg looks like a "0." When the game was imported into England from France the term was also introduced, but its spelling was changed to "love." We sometimes call a zero a "goose egg."

Low Road. *What are the "high road" and the "low road" in the song "Loch Lomond"?*

The "high road" is the highway, of course; but the term "low road" refers to an old Celtic belief that when a man meets his death in a foreign land, his spirit returns to the place of his birth by an underground fairy way—by the "low road." The song tells of two wounded Scottish soldiers, held prisoners in the Carlisle jail. One of them was to be released; he would take the "high road" home to Scotland. The other was to be executed; he would take the "low road." But the dead man, traveling by the "low road" with the speed of a spirit, would naturally—or supernaturally—be in Scotland before the living, who would have to tramp the many weary miles of the "high road" before he could hope to reach Scotland. It is this thought which consoles the Scot singing as he is about to die.

Lumber. *What is the origin of the word "lumber"?*

Since the first pawnbrokers came from Lombardi, Italy, their shops were called "Lombard Shops." Pawnbrokers generally have a great many odds and ends lying about their shops taking up space—and so any space-filling miscellany was called "Lombard." In time the word became "lumber." Since the sawed timber, barrel staves and ship masts left lying around in the dealer's yard take up a lot of room the yard was called a "lumber yard." From this the timber itself came to be called "lumber."

Lump It. *How did the word "lump" get into the expression "if you don't like it you can lump it"?*

A person's face will often look "lumpy" after crying. So to "lump it" is to sulk or look sulky—and the phrase "like it or lump it" means "like it or sulk."

Lurch. *Where did we get the expression "left in the lurch"?*

The expression comes to us from the game of cribbage. The game is marked by inserting pegs in two rows of holes in a board, one after the other, as the player makes a fresh score. Once up and down the board completes a game. If one player has gone up and down the board before the other has finished going up, he wins what is called a "lurch" or double game—and his opponent, left so far behind, has been "left in the lurch."

Lush. *Why do we call a drunkard a "lush"?*

"The City of Lushington" was the name of a convivial society made up chiefly of actors that met at the Harp Tavern in London until about 1895. The society had a "Lord Mayor" and four "aldermen"—from "wards" named "Juniper," "Poverty," "Lunacy," and "Suicide." It was the duty of the "Lord Mayor" to lecture new members on the evils of drink. A member of this society was known as a "lush."

Lynch. *What is the origin of the term "lynch law"?*

Charles Lynch was a Justice of the Peace of Bedford County, Virginia, in 1780 when gangs of Loyalists were ravaging the countryside—more like robbers than like men fighting for a cause. Many of these men were captured—but at that time the only court in Virginia authorized to try felonies was in Williamsburg and Lynch and his colleagues of the Magistrate's Court of Bedford County discovered that the Loyalists sent to Williamsburg for trial were rescued before they reached that city. So they set up a rump court of their own and proceeded to try their prisoners. Though they kept strictly to legal forms in these trials, the setting up of the court itself was unlawful. But Lynch and his associates accomplished their end and put down much of the prevailing lawlessness. Fines were heavy and corporal punishment was often inflicted—but the only person to be hanged was a Negro slave convicted of poisoning his master's wife. The present meaning of the term "lynch law" grew with the development of its practice until today a "lynching" is almost always a hanging without any trial at all.

Macaroni. *Why did Yankee Doodle call himself "macaroni"?*

Because that was the then current name for a "fop" or a "dandy." It was the name for a dandy because a group of well-traveled young Englishmen of wealth and position formed a club called the "Macaroni Club" in London, around 1760. They named the club that because they were fond of foreign cooking. These young men also dressed in a foreign manner; the common people misunderstood the use of the word "macaroni" and took the name of their club to be descriptive of their dress.

McCoy. *What is the reason we use the phrase "the real McCoy" to mean "genuine"?*

This term became popular because of a story that attained wide circulation. A prize fighter by the name of McCoy was being annoyed by a drunk. The pest wanted McCoy to fight but, being a professional boxer and realizing the man's condition, McCoy refused. Friends tried to calm down the drunk by telling him that the man he was annoying was the famous prize fighter, McCoy; the drunk didn't believe them and finally became so annoying that McCoy punched him and knocked him out. When he came to, the drunk said, "You're right; he's the real McCoy!"

Machiavellian. *How did the word "machiavellian" come to mean "evil"?*

Niccolo Machiavelli of Florence wrote a book called "The Prince." It expounded the art of government and showed how by treachery and other despicable acts it was possible for a prince to achieve and uphold arbitrary power.

Mackinaw. *Where did the "mackinaw" get that name?*

The term was first applied to the gaudy blankets issued by the Government in the 1820's and used in Indian trade, especially at the trading post of Mackinac, Michigan—which had been named *Mitchimakinak* by the Ojibway Indians. The jackets were first made of this colorful blanket cloth; and since "Mackinac" is pronounced "Mackinaw," they were called "Mackinaw" jackets.

Mad as a March Hare. *Why do we say "mad as a March hare"?*

March begins the rutting season for hares and the hares run about wildly at that time—apparently quite "mad."

Magazine. *What is the reason a periodical is called a "magazine"?*

Because it's considered a storehouse for numerous articles. The term comes from *makhzan*, the Arabic word for "storehouse," and was originally applied to a place used

160

by the Army for storing arms. "Magazine" was first used in its present sense in 1731 when "The Gentleman's Magazine" appeared.

Magenta. *Why is the color "magenta" called that?*
The color got its name from the Battle of Magenta, fought in 1859. The color was discovered shortly afterwards and was named to commemorate the battle.

Maintain. *What is the origin of the word "maintain"?*
This word is from the Latin *manu tenere*—which literally means to "hold with the hand." It is descriptive of "holding one's own."

Make the Bed. *Why do we say we "make" a bed when we spread the sheets and blankets?*
We speak of "making" the bed, instead of "fixing" it or "doing" it because beds were once created anew each night from straw thrown upon the floor.

Make No Bones. *How did the expression "make no bones about it" come to mean frank speech?*
The early meaning of this expression was "to let things pass"; a guest finding a bone in his fish soup or chowder would, for politeness' sake, "make no [mention of the] bones." Then the phrase began to be used in a satiric sense to mean just the opposite. Now the original meaning has been almost forgotten.

Make One's Mark. *Why do we say a person who has achieved success has "made his mark" in the world?*
At one time smiths and other artisans had distinctive marks which they placed upon their wares. If the artisan's mark became generally known, he had "made his

mark in the world." The idea of a person's "making his mark"—that is, placing his name—on the pages of history is of later origin.

Man on Horseback. *How did a dictator get the name "man on horseback" applied to him?*

The famous dictator of France, General Ernest Boulanger, made almost all his public appearances on horseback—and so we apply the phrase to any dictator.

Manna. *Where did "manna" get that name?*

From the Israelites who first saw this "food" spread upon the ground. From the Biblical description of manna we can deduce that it was hail; but the Israelites did not know what it was—and so they exclaimed *"Man-hu"*—which, translated literally, means: "What is it?"

Mansard Roof. *What is the origin of the "mansard roof"?*

Paris in the eleventh century limited the number of floors to a building. The French architect, Francois Mansard, got around this law by lifting up parts of the roof and giving the house, in effect, an extra story.

Mantelpiece. *How did the "mantelpiece" get its name?*

From the fact that it once was just a shelf over a fireplace on which coats, cloaks and "mantles" were hung to dry.

Many a Slip. *Why do we say that there's "many a slip 'twixt the cup and the lip"?*

The expression is an allusion to the legend of the slave of Ankaios, the helmsman of the Argo, who told his master that he would never taste the wine which came from his own vineyard. He was right. Just as Ankaios was ready to lift the cup to his lip he heard that a wild boar was wreaking havoc in his vineyard. Ankaios rushed out and the boar killed him.

Mardi Gras. *Where did the "Mardi Gras" get that name?*

The term is French and literally means "fat Tuesday." It got its name from the French custom of parading a fat ox as part of the celebration of the day.

Married at the Church Door. *What is the origin of the expression "married at the church door"?*

The phrase was once literally true. Some five hundred years ago it was the custom in England to perform the wedding ceremony at the door of the church. After it was over, the couple entered the church for Mass. Later, the ceremony was moved inside for communicants of the church; only when one of the parties to the marriage was a Protestant, or divorced, or otherwise undesirable was the ceremony performed at the door.

Martinet. *Where did the "martinet" get that name?*

From a commander of the French infantry. In the reign of Louis XIV of France, General Martinet remodeled the French infantry by instituting very strict discipline based upon severe punishment—so severe that the French call a cat-o'-nine-tails a "martinet," and the English adopted the term as a synonym for a strict disciplinarian.

Maru. *Why do all Japanese ships have the word "maru" as a part of their name?*

"Maru" has been attached to the names of Japanese ships for thousands of years. The word means "perfect" or

163

"complete." According to the old legend, in ancient China some 4,000 years ago a fair messenger was sent down from Heaven to Lord Takao-Tzu to teach him the art of shipbuilding. The messenger's name was Hakudo Maru. In deference to this celestial shipbuilding instructor, Japanese ships bear the suffix *"maru."*

Masher. *How did the "masher" get that name?*
This term, like "crush," has the connotation of a strong embrace—one that "mashes"; it's influenced, however, by the Gypsy word for one who entices or fascinates, *masha.*

Maudlin. *What is the reason an over-sentimental person is said to be "maudlin"?*
The term is an impious reference to Mary Magdalene— a British pronunciation of Magdalene being "maudlin," as in Magdalene College. Medieval painters represented Mary Magdalene as having a very doleful face, her eyes swollen with weeping.

Maverick. *Where did stray cattle get the name "mavericks"?*
In Texas—where, about 1840, one Samuel Maverick began raising cattle. Maverick failed to brand any of his calves—which led to wholesale rustling of Maverick stock. From this, any unbranded animal came to be called a "maverick."

Mealy-Mouthed. *Why do we say a sweet-speaking person is "mealy-mouthed"?*
Because "mealy-mouthed" is just an improper pronunciation of the Greek *melimuthos*—and *meli* means "honey" while *muthos* means "speech."

164

Melancholy. *How did we get the word "melancholy"?*

The term comes from the Greek *melaina,* meaning "black," and *chole,* meaning "bile." The early Greeks thought that the emotions were made active by the bile —and that a sorrowful feeling was created by a "black bile."

Mentor. *Why is a mental or moral guide called a "mentor"?*

"Mentor" was the name of a faithful friend of Ulysses whose form Minerva assumed when she accompanied Telemachus in his search for his father. And so, the term means a "wise counselor and guide."

Mikado. *Is "Mikado" the title of the Emperor of Japan?*

Not at all. And only by inference does it refer to a person who lives at the imperial palace. The term comes from the Japanese *mi,* meaning "august," and *kado,* meaning "door." Behind this "august door" lived the Emperor; but no Japanese would think of mentioning him by any name—and so they refer to his door instead.

Milliner. *What is the origin of the word "milliner"?*

At one time the city of Milan set the fashion throughout the world—much as Paris did at a later date. The "Milaner" was, therefore, a stylist—whence, "milliner."

Minister. *How did a "minister" come to be called that?*

The word literally means an "inferior person" or "servant." The original idea was that a minister was supposed to serve his parishioners. This idea has not yet completely disappeared.

Minutes of a Meeting. *Why are the notes of a meeting called "minutes"?*

Because these notes are made in "minute" or small writing—that is, in shorthand.

Miscreant. *Where do we get the word "miscreant"?*

The term is from the French *mescreant*, and literally means an "unbeliever." It was first applied by the Christians to the Mohammedans—who in turn called the Christians "infidels"—since neither side believed the other followed the "true" religion.

Missouri. *What is the reason we say "I'm from Missouri; you'll have to show me"?*

The expression was popularized by Colonel Vandiver, Representative in Congress from Missouri. But it probably originated in the mining town of Leadville, Colorado, where men migrated from Missouri to work in the mines. Because these men were new on the job, the pit bosses constantly said, "That man is from Missouri; you'll have to show him."

Mollycoddle. *How did a weak person come to be called a "mollycoddle"?*

"Molly" is a familiar pet form of "Mary" which was once contemptuously applied to a wench or prostitute. (It still is in the term "gangster's moll.") This contemptuous use led people to call an effeminate man a "Molly" —and to "mollycoddle" yourself is to take as much care of yourself as such a one would.

166

Monkey Jacket. *Why do we call a mess jacket a "monkey jacket"?*

No reference to the organ grinder's "monkey" is intended. A "monkey jacket" is one without tails—and so more properly should be termed an "ape jacket." The name was first applied to the short jacket worn by sailors.

Monkey-Wrench. *Where did the "monkey-wrench" get that name?*

According to tradition this wrench with a movable jaw adjustable by a screw was first made by a London blacksmith named Charles Moncke and the tool was originally called a "Moncke-wrench" in his honor—just as a "Stillson-wrench" today bears the name of its inventor. But since few people knew the true origin of the word, it was soon corrupted into "monkey-wrench."

Moron. *What is the origin of the word "moron"?*

The term is pure Greek but was arbitrarily given to adults with a mental age of eight to twelve years by Dr. Henry H. Goddard. Classifying the mentality of subnormal people into three groups, those with the lowest intellect would quite obviously be called "idiots" and the middle group, "imbeciles"—but the highest group needed a new name. So Dr. Goddard picked out of his Greek lexicon the word *moron*, meaning "dull, stupid, silly, foolish"—all of which he felt to be a perfect description of this group.

Morris Chair. *Is the "Morris chair" in any way related to the "morris dance"?*

Not at all. William Morris, the English artist, gave his name to the chair—though he did not, as so many believe, invent it. The "morris dance" got its name from its inventors—the Moors who conquered Spain. It was originally called a "Moorish dance."

Mosey. *How did "mosey" come to mean a slow walk?*

The term comes from the Spanish *vamose*, meaning "let's go." We've preserved the word in its entirety to indicate rapid travel—in the form of "vamoose"—and we have taken the last syllable and use it to mean slow travel.

Mother Carey's Chickens. *Where did the birds known as "Mother Carey's chickens" get that name?*

The French speak of these birds as "the birds of our Mother St. Mary." Another phrase applied to them is the Latin form for "dear mother"—*mater cara*. This sounds like "Mother Carey" and was so translated by British sailors.

Mother Earth. *Why do we speak of the Earth as "great Mother Earth"?*

Among almost all peoples the Earth was at one time reverenced as the "mother" of all. The Romans, for instance, tell the story of how the two sons of Tarquinius, together with Junius Brutus, asked the Delphic Oracle which one of them would succeed to the throne of Rome. The oracle replied, "He who shall first kiss his mother." The two sons of Tarquinius raced home to find their mother but Junius Brutus fell to the ground saying, "Thus I kiss thee, oh Earth, great mother of us all." He became king.

Mountebank. *What is the reason a "mountebank" is so called?*

Street venders once used a counter known as a "bank"—from the Italian name for it, *banca*—and they used to "mount" on this "bank" to cry their wares to the public.

Mud in Your Eye. *How did "here's mud in your eye" come to be an accepted toast?*

The expression is not a toast to another; it is a toast to yourself—for it means, "I hope I beat you." The allusion is to a horse race. If the track is at all muddy the rider of the losing horse is very likely to get mud in his eye from the horse that is winning.

Mufti. *Where did we get the word "mufti" to describe casual clothes?*

Indirectly from the Arabic. A Mohammedan priest is called a *mufti* and his clothes aren't at all like ours. In the early nineteenth century, English music hall comedians represented the Army officer off duty as wearing a dressing gown and smoking cap and slippers—and since this dress was not the usual garb of an officer they called him a "mufti." The officers themselves picked up the term and started calling their undress clothes "mufti."

Mug. *Why do we use the word "mug" to mean our face?*

Because a comparatively small jug used for drinking is called a "mug" and in the eighteenth century in England these "mugs" were commonly made to represent a human face.

169

Mugwump. *What is the origin of the term "mugwump"?*

"Mugwump" is an Algonquin Indian word meaning "chief," but John Elliot in his famous Indian Bible of 1663 used it as an equivalent of the word "duke." "Mugwump" was first used as a term of derision in the Presidential campaign of 1884 where it was applied to those Republicans of means and consequence who refused to support James G. Blaine for the Presidency.

Mumblety-Peg. *How did the game of "mumblety-peg" get that name?*

The name of the game is correctly "mumble-the-peg." The loser is required to pull out of the ground with his teeth a "peg" which has been driven in with a certain number of blows of the knife handle. The loser, in his attempts to get the peg, makes sounds like a person "mumbling."

Muscle. *Where did we get the word "muscle"?*

From the Latin *musculus*, which means "little mouse." If you move the "muscles" of your upper arm you will see what looks like a little mouse crawling back and forth.

Mushy. *Why is the word "mush" used in describing the feeling of love?*

The term was originally and more appropriately applied to kisses. Kisses that are wet are called "mushy"—for they leave the same moisture around the mouth that is found on the face of a small child after he has been fed "mush."

170

QUIZ 6

(Answers on page 276)

1. Why do we call a scholarly person "high-brow"?
2. How did "mother-of-pearl" get that name?
3. Where does the term "square shooter" come from?
4. Why do we call an insane person a "lunatic"?
5. What is the origin of the expression "like greased lightning"?
6. How did we come to call making much of a person "lionizing" him?
7. Why do we say a meaningful remark is "pithy"?
8. How did something very fine come to be called "gilt-edged"?
9. What is the origin of the expression "la-di-da"?
10. Why is a person who is feeling good said to be feeling "chipper"?
11. How did the giraffe come to be called a "cameleopard"?
12. Why do we call a small child a "shaver"?
13. What is the origin of the word "automobile"?
14. How did a thin person come to be called "spindling"?
15. Why do we use the term "milksop" to mean a weakling?
16. How did a small, sleepy town come to be called a "backwater" village?
17. What is the origin of the expression "I don't care a hang"?
18. Why do we say a plain-spoken person is "downright" frank?
19. What is the origin of the term "lingo"?
20. Why do we call a person in love "moon-struck"?

```
N N N N N N
N         N
N    N    N
N    A    N
N N N N N N
```

Nail One's Colors to the Mast. *Where does the expression "nail one's colors to the mast" come from?*

From naval warfare. In a battle at sea a ship surrenders by striking its colors—that is, lowering its flag. If the colors are "nailed to the mast" they cannot be lowered and the ship cannot surrender; it must fight on no matter what happens.

Naked Truth. *Why do we call absolute truth "the naked truth"?*

Because, according to ancient legend, Truth and Falsehood once went bathing. When they came out of the water, Falsehood ran ahead, dressed herself in Truth's clothing, and sped away. Truth, unwilling to appear in Falsehood's clothing, went "naked."

Narrow-Back. *How did a dandy come to be called a "narrow-back"?*

The Irishmen who came to this country all wore the rough-cut, homespun clothes of their homeland but their sons adopted the practice of wearing tailor-made clothes that were cut to fit. The coats, therefore, were cut in at the waist and gave the men a "narrow-back" appearance.

172

Neat as a New Pin. *What is the reason "neat as a new pin" means extremely neat?*

In the days before pins were made of brass or tin coated, they were made of iron wire and rusted quickly. Only a new pin was without blemish.

Necking. *From what did the word "necking" get its current meaning?*

From the neck's being an added object of the affection and the theoretical lower limit of action. The word "neck" itself has its origin in the Dutch *nekken*, meaning "to kill." Our neck acquired its name from the fact that you pull or twist the neck of a chicken to kill it. But there's no implied allusion to this origin in the current meaning of "necking."

Needle. *Where did we get the expression "give him the needle"?*

The term comes from a tailor's practical joke. When a group of tailors are sitting on the table side by side, one tailor will take his needle and slyly jab another in the rear. The startled reaction of the victim of this practical joke is considered by many to be very funny.

Nemesis. *Why do we call something that pursues a man relentlessly his "nemesis"?*

Because in Greek mythology "Nemesis" was an avenging goddess who saw to it that people were punished for their misdeeds. In Greek *nemesis* really means "remorse."

173

Nest Egg. *How did something put by for an emergency get the name "nest egg"?*

It was once a common practice, when collecting eggs from a hen roost, to leave behind a single egg in each nest —so that the hen would continue to lay. From this, "nest egg" got the meaning of something laid by to take care of the future. It's interesting to note that this practice, though no longer necessary with barnyard fowl, is still effective with other birds. Once a bird starts to lay, it will usually continue laying long enough to put the normal number of eggs for its species in the nest. An experiment on one songbird, in which each day all but one egg was removed from the nest, led to the production of seventy-two eggs—though the usual clutch was less than a half-dozen.

Nick of Time. *How did we get the expression "in the nick of time"?*

In medieval days a "tally" was used to register attendance in colleges and churches. The "tally" was a stick of wood and attendance was indicated by a "nick" or notch on it. The student or worshipper who arrived in time had his attendance "nicked"—and so arrived "in the nick of time."

Nine Days' Wonder. *Where did the phrase "nine days' wonder" come from?*

This expression originally referred to the novena of the Roman Catholic Church—and "novena" comes from the Latin *novenus*, meaning "nine each." The patron saint of each church is accorded a novena which lasts for nine days—during which time the image of the saint, relics and other sacred objects are paraded for the "wonder" or veneration of the worshippers.

Niobe's Tears. *What is the origin of the term "Niobe's tears"?*

The synonym for "perpetual weeping" comes from Greek mythology. Niobe, Queen of Thebes, was the mother of seven sons and seven daughters and a vain woman indeed. When the people of Thebes gathered for their annual celebration of the feast of the goddess Latona, Niobe appeared and told them to worship her instead—for she was queen and had seven times as many children as Latona. They obeyed. Latona became indignant and asked her children, Apollo and Diana, to help restore her prestige in the eyes of the people. Angered at

175

the slight to their mother, they flew to the city of Thebes and slew all the fourteen children of Niobe with bows and arrows. In spite of her grief, the Queen continued to berate Latona; thereupon she was changed to stone—yet "Niobe's tears" continued to flow. She was finally borne upon a wind to her native mountain where she still remains—a mass of rock from which a trickling stream flows, product of her never-ending grief.

Nose to the Grindstone. *How did we come to say a busy man "keeps his nose to the grindstone"?*
A man who is very busy literally and figuratively "humps himself"—he bends over. This brings his nose forward; and if he's busy grinding, it makes him appear to be grinding his own nose.

Nostrum. *What is the reason we call a quack medicine a "nostrum"?*
Nostrum is a Latin word meaning "of us" or "ours." The quacks of the Middle Ages—who used puppets and acrobats to attract crowds and help them sell their medicines—refused to divulge their contents or formula, saying "it's ours"—"*nostrum.*"

Nuts in May. *Where is the sense in the expression "here we go gathering nuts in May"?*
Not "nuts" at all—"knots"; in other words, "sprigs of flowers." These do come out in May.

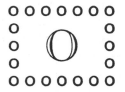

Oats. *Why do we say that a youth who's acting the gay young blade is "feeling his oats" or "sowing his wild oats"?*

It's because feeding oats to a horse makes him lively. When a horse begins to prance around he's "feeling his oats." And when he finds wild oats in the pasture and eats them, and then, feeling these oats, starts gadding about he will literally as well as figuratively "sow his wild oats."

Oil on Troubled Waters. *What is the reason we speak of pacifying someone as "pouring oil on troubled waters"?*

Because it's a scientific fact that oil poured on a rough sea will lessen the waves. Benjamin Franklin, on hearing this Biblical phrase repeated, decided to test its literal truth. He poured oil on the ocean and found the waves were considerably reduced.

O.K. *Where did we get the expression "O.K."?*

From the Presidential election of 1840. The Democratic candidate, Martin Van Buren, was nicknamed "The Wizard of Kinderhook"—after "Old Kinderhook," the Hudson Valley village in which he had been born. In reference to this village and Van Buren's nickname one of the Democratic groups formed to support him in New York City called itself "The Democratic O.K. Club." Other supporters of Van Buren in New York picked up the term "O.K." as a sort of slogan, and Democratic rowdies used it as their war cry in their attempts to break up meetings of Whigs. The phrase caught on generally and soon established itself as synonymous with the feeling of the original club members that they and their candidates were "all right."

On the Carpet. *How did "on the carpet" come to mean a reprimand?*

Originally, only the boss's office had a "carpet"; the other offices didn't. So, to be called "on the carpet" was to be called into the boss's office—and this usually meant a reprimand.

On the Cuff. *Why do we say that something purchased and charged is put "on the cuff"?*

Because it was once the custom of waiters in public houses to keep a record of what was ordered on the cuffs of their shirts. For this reason, a diner who wished to have his meal charged would jocularly suggest that the amount due be put "on the cuff" also.

On the Level. *Where did we get the expression "on the level"?*

The term originated in Freemasonry. The level is an emblem of that organization—as is the square—and the Masons first used "on the level" as well as "on the square" to refer to the other Masons.

178

On the Spot. *Why do we say that a man murdered by gangsters was put "on the spot"?*

The "spot" referred to is the prearranged place for the murder—and the surest way to get a victim there is to "put" him there.

On Tick. *How did we come to call charging a purchase "buying on tick"?*

In the seventeenth century "ticket" was the standard term for a "due bill" or written acknowledgment of a debt. "On tick," therefore, means "on the ticket"—that is, by promissory note rather than by cash.

Ordeal. *Where does the word "ordeal" come from?*

From the Old English word *adaelan*, meaning "to deal out." From this idea of giving to each his share, "ordeal" came to mean "judgment." It was once the custom to try a man by subjecting him to torture—in the belief that God would defend the right, even by a miracle. This form of judgment by torture was called an "ordeal" —whence the present meaning of the word.

Ostracize. *Why do we say a person who's kept out of a group is "ostracized"?*

The word comes from the Greek *ostrakon*, meaning a "tile." It was the custom in ancient Greece to send into exile for five or ten years a person whose power or influence was considered dangerous to the state. This decree of banishment was effected by taking a vote on the question—and the voting was done with tiles on which the person's name was written.

179

Ouija Board. *How did the "ouija board" get that name?*
"Ouija" means "yes, yes." The name is a compound of
the French *oui* and the German *ja* and no doubt is derived from the fact that the "ouija board" agrees with its
operators; it is a mechanical "yes man."

Ovation. *Where did we get the word "ovation" as the
name for "triumphant acclaim"?*
From the Romans. But the Roman "ovation" was only
a "second-class" celebration for a lesser triumph—a battle
won without bloodshed or a victory over slaves. The
honored citizen did not appear in a chariot but only on
a horse or on foot.

P P P P P P P
P P P
P P P
P P P
P P P P P P P

Paddle Your Own Canoe. *Where does the expression "paddle your own canoe" come from?*

The phrase was first used in a poem published in "Harper's Magazine" for May, 1854.

> " Leave to Heaven, in humble trust,
> All you will to do
> But if you would succeed, you must
> Paddle your own canoe."

Paddywhack. *Why do we call a light spank a "paddywhack"?*

The Irish call St. Patrick, their patron saint, *Padraig*—and so an Irishman is called a "Paddy." Irish comedians in the English theater were very partial to the "slapstick"—and so a "paddywhack" is a harmless slap on the buttocks in jest.

Pagan. *How did a "pagan" get that name?*

The Christian Church made its first converts in the cities, its next in the villages and its last in the country. "Pagan" is from the Latin *pagus* and literally means "belonging to a village."

Pain. *What is the origin of the word "pain"?*

This word literally means "punishment." It's from the Latin *poena*, meaning "penalty." The original idea must have been that anyone who suffers pain must deserve punishment—for Adam's sins, if not for his own.

Palace. *Where did we get the word "palace"?*

From Rome—for the word originally meant a dwelling on the "Palatine" Hill in Rome. Augustus built his home there—and so did Tiberius and Nero.

Pale. *Why do we say an uncouth person or act is "beyond the pale"?*

In the twelfth century, when the English first went into Ireland, they established themselves in the region around Dublin. This was known as the "pale." English authority existed only "within the pale" and the remainder of Ireland was governed by local kings and leaders of clans, some of whom were regarded as very uncouth. So "beyond the pale" came to mean outside of the "civilized" zone of British jurisdiction.

Pall Mall. *How did "Pall Mall" get its name; and why is it pronounced "Pell Mell"?*

In the Italian game of ball called *palamaglio*, the players run about in apparent reckless confusion. When this game was introduced into England, it was called "pall-mall"—from the Italian *palla* meaning "ball" and *maglio* meaning "mallet." Though the English spelled the name "Pall Mall" when they named the playing ground—and later the street and park—after the game, they pronounced it "Pell Mell"—from their "pell-mell" manner

182

of playing it. "Pell-mell" itself is from the French *pêsle-mêsle*—the *pêsle* being just rhyming duplication for emphasis. *Mêsle* means "mix."

Pallbearer. *Why is a "pallbearer" called that?*
The Romans called the square piece of cloth they threw over their shoulders a *pallium*—and so any sort of covering is a "pall." "Pallbearers" once carried the coffin under a "pall"—though today this coffin covering is not widely used.

Palm It Off. *What is the reason getting rid of something by passing it on to another is called "palming it off"?*
The expression comes from card playing. If a cardshark, about to deal a card to himself, discovers (by peeking) that it's one he doesn't like he may hide it in the palm of his hand and deal himself another. Then he will "palm off" the first card to one of the other players.

Pan Out. *Where did we get the expression "pan out"?*
It's a gold mining term. One method of obtaining gold dust is to take a handful or so of the sand in which it's found and place it with a little water in a "pan." Then, by sloshing the water back and forth, the lighter sand, dirt, and pebbles can be sluiced over the edge while the gold dust, which is heavier, will remain behind in the pan—and so "pan out."

Panic. *Why do we call sudden widespread fear "panic"?*
Sounds heard on the mountain tops and in the deep valleys at night were once attributed to the god, "Pan"—he was believed to be the cause of any sudden, groundless fear—and so such a fear was called "panic."

183

Pants. *What is the reason trousers are called "pants"?*

The term is just a shortened form of "pantaloons"—the name of the ridiculous baggy trousers worn by a character in the Italian *commedia dell 'arte* who was the butt of all jokes. This character was known as the *pantalone* —after the patron saint of Venice, San Pantaleone—because the name in its Greek form means "all lion" and he was meek and mild. Drooping pants are still used in the theater for comic effect.

Paraphernalia. *How did personal belongings come to be called "paraphernalia"?*

According to Roman law there were certain things which a wife might claim as hers upon the death of her husband—articles that weren't a part of her dower. The Romans adopted a Greek word to cover these items, *parapherna,* meaning "beside dower."

Pariah. *Why do we call a despised social' outcast a "pariah"?*

Because the "pariah" of India belongs to one of the lowest castes of Hindu society. He gets his name from the Timbal word for "drummer," *paraiyan*—because he plays the drums at Hindu festivals.

Parlor. *How did the "parlor" get its name?*

"Parlor" comes from the French *parler,* meaning "to speak"—it's really a "conversation room" in which you entertain your guests. "Drawing room" is short for "withdrawing room"—the room to which you withdraw after a meal.

184

Parthian Shot. *Why do we use the term "Parthian shot" to indicate a final thrust as one departs?*

Because that's how the Parthians fought. They used to charge on horseback at their enemies, shooting arrows at them. But then, instead of stopping to fight, they'd ride away again—shooting arrows till out of range.

Pass the Buck. *What is the origin of the expression "pass the buck"?*

In an old English card game a jacknife—or "buck"—was passed from player to player to show whose turn it was to chip in. The procedure was adopted in poker and a "buck" was passed from player to player to indicate whose turn it was to deal—and, as dealer, add a chip to the pot. Since only the dealer could stack or juggle the cards, to "pass the buck" came to mean to "pass on responsibility for an honest deal."

Paul Pry. *Where did a "nosey" person get the name "Paul Pry"?*

It's from a play by John Poole—a comedy about an inquisitive meddler named Paul Pry. Pry always came on stage with the apology, "I hope I don't interrupt."

Pay the Piper. *Why do we use the phrase "pay the piper" to indicate future remorse?*

Because, though dancing is fun, still the "piper" who leads the dance—or plays for it—has to be "paid." The moral is pointed out in the story of the Pied Piper of Hamlin—who wasn't paid for ridding the town of rats and so led the town children away.

185

Pea Jacket. *How did the "pea jacket" that sailors wear get that name?*

The term is derived from the Dutch *pig* or *pije*, meaning "coarse thick cloth or felt"—and refers to the cloth used in making the "pea jackets." A sailor's jacket is sometimes called a "reefer" because it is close-fitting and pulled in tight—like a sail that has been reefed.

Pedagogue. *Where does the word "pedagogue" come from?*

From the Romans. In Rome, a "pedagogue" was a slave who took the children to school, to the theater, and on their outings—although he often taught them as well. The word comes from the Greek *paid*, meaning "child," and *agein*, meaning "to lead."

Peeping Tom. *Why do we call a person who makes a practice of peeping a "peeping Tom"?*

It's because the tailor who tried to get a look at Lady Godiva as she rode naked through the streets of Coventry—in an attempt to obtain a reduction of the taxes imposed upon the people—was named "Tom." This particular "peeping Tom" was struck blind.

Petticoat. *What is the reason a woman's underskirt is called a "petticoat"?*

Originally the garment was a "petty coat"—a small coat worn by men under their coat of mail or doublet. Then women adopted the garment—they too wore a short or "petty" coat. But in time they lengthened the garment and lowered its support until it reached from the waist to below their knees.

186

Phaeton. *How did the carriage get the name "phaeton"?*
The carriage was named for the god, Phaethon, son of Apollo, who tried to drive the chariot of the Sun. He did not succeed—the chariot tipped over.

Philadelphia Lawyer. *Where did we get the expression "Philadelphia lawyer"?*
This term originated at a time when the Philadelphia bar was distinguished for its acuteness and professional skill. In the first great contest in America over the freedom of the press, John Peter Zenger was sued for libel by William Crosby, the colonial governor, because of criticisms he had published in the "New York Weekly Journal." Andrew Hamilton, a Philadelphia lawyer, defended him and won a complete acquittal on the grounds that the criticisms offered were statements of fact. A great deal of attention was called at that time to the fact that it took a "Philadelphia lawyer" to win a case in New York.

Philander. *What is the reason a person inconstant in love is said to "philander"?*
The word literally means "loving man." It's from the Greek *philos*, meaning "loving," and *andros*, meaning "man." In the ballad, "The Faithful Lover's Downfall," the girl, Phillis, kills herself because she loses her man, "Philander," to another.

Philippic. *Why do we call a verbal attack a "philippic"?*
Demosthenes attempted to arouse the Athenians to resistance against Philip of Macedon. His orations against "Philip" are "Philippics"—hence this name for a strong speech by one person attacking another.

187

Philosopher. *How did the "philosopher" come to be called that?*

The Greek word for "wise" is *sophos*—and the sages of Greece were once called that. But Pythagoras thought this word too arrogant and so added the word *philos*, meaning "loving." The *philos-sophos*, or "philosopher," is therefore a "lover of wisdom."

Phoney. *Where did we get the word "phoney" as a synonym for "spurious"?*

From an American manufacturer of cheap jewelry named Forney. Forney made a specialty of brass rings which looked like gold. He sold these rings by the barrelful to street peddlers and soon the rings came to be known by them as "Forney rings." The pronunciation was in time changed to "phoney" and the word was extended to apply to other forms of jewelry—and eventually to anything that was fraudulent.

Pickaninny. *Do the words "ninny" and "pickaninny" have anything in common?*

Not a thing. "Ninny" is a diminutive of "nincompoop"; "pickaninny" comes from the Spanish *pequeno*, meaning "little child."

Pig in a Poke. *What is the reason we refer to buying something sight unseen as "buying a pig in a poke"?*

A "poke" is a bag—from the Irish word for it, *poc*. It was once the custom to bring small pigs to market in a bag. And if you bought such a "pig in a poke" without looking at it you didn't really know what you were getting.

188

Pig Iron. *How did "pig iron" come to be called that?*

Molten iron from a blast furnace is run into molds dug in the sand; these molds are a series of parallel trenches connected by a channel which runs at right angles to them—and the whole looks something like a sow with a litter of suckling pigs.

Pigeon English. *Where did "pigeon English" get that name?*

The "pigeon" of "pigeon English" is pigeon English for "business." It was derived in this manner: bidjiness, bidjin, pidgin, pidgeon, and finally, pigeon.

Pigeonhole. *Why is one of a tier of compartments called a "pigeonhole"?*

Because a dovecot—the home of domesticated pigeons—is usually divided up into many little compartments, each one, literally, a "pigeon hole."

Piker. *What is the reason we call a poor sport who hates to spend money a "piker"?*

The English once called a tramp or vagrant a "piker" because he tramped the "turnpike." The man who's a poor sport and won't spend any money is like the tramp who hasn't any and can't; therefore, he has been given the same name, "piker."

Pillar to Post. *How did we come to say a person is tossed about "from pillar to post"?*

The expression refers to the fact that at one time an offender against law and order was either placed in the pillory or whipped at the whipping post—and sometimes was forced to go from one to the other.

189

Pin Money. *What is the origin of the term "pin money"?*

When pins were introduced at the beginning of the six-teenth century they were made of silver and considered quite a luxury. For this reason they were used as gifts on New Year's Day. In time, instead of giving his wife a gift of pins, the husband merely gave her the money to buy the pins. Then the term was extended to signify the sum of money a man gave his wife each year—or upon their marriage—for her private expenses. And, finally, "pin money" became recognized in law and a wife could sue to collect—but only for one year's "pin money."

Pinchbeck. *How did the "pinchbeck" bottle get its name?*

A "pinchbeck" bottle, or other object, is a showy one. The name comes to us from one Christopher Pinchbeck, a London watchmaker, who invented an alloy of copper and zinc that looked like gold.

Platform. *What is the reason we call a political party's statement of its aims a "platform"?*

A political candidate must appear before his constituents in order to win their votes. To be seen and heard he must stand upon a platform. The platform is constructed of planks. From this, the statement of political faith upon which he stands—or falls—is called a "platform" and its various parts are known as "planks."

Pleased as Punch. *Why do we say we're "as pleased as punch"?*

Because, in the standard "Punch and Judy" show, "Punch" carries a stick with which he belabors "Judy" —and then bursts into screams of laughter.

190

Plebes. *How did the freshmen at Annapolis come to be called "plebes"?*

The students at the United States Naval Academy at Annapolis started calling the first-year men "plebes" as a shortened form of "plebeian," which comes from the Latin word for the "common people." "Freshmen," of course, just means new or "fresh" men.

Plucky. *What is the reason we call a brave man "plucky"?*

The "pluck" is that which is "plucked" from the innards of a bird or an animal preparatory to serving it at the table—the heart, gizzard, liver, and guts. A "plucky" man is one who has "guts"—and we use both terms to mean emotional stamina and stability.

Plus Fours. *How did golfers' short pants come to be called "plus fours"?*

Ordinary knickerbockers, or knee-breeches, were not full enough at the knees to allow a full swing in playing golf. So, in making golf knickers, four inches were added to the length of the seam to allow the knickers to hang over the knees and thus give the player enough slack. The tailor's notation for this was "+4."

Point Blank. *Where did we get the expression "point blank"?*

From the French. The center of a target was once a small white spot and the French for "white" is *blanc*. The French *point* means "aim." So the term literally means, "aim at the center of the target." "Point blank range" is a range so short you can hardly miss a bull's-eye.

Poke Bonnet. *Why is a "poke bonnet" called that?*

This bonnet got its name from the fact that the front of it "poked out" far beyond the face. A bonnet that didn't do so was called a "kiss-me-quick."

Poker. *How did the game of "poker" get that name?*

The game is German in origin and gets its name from the German *pochen,* meaning "to boast" or "brag"—though a literal translation is "to knock." A "knock" is still used in poker to indicate a passed bet—and the game still includes considerable "bragging." But the game seems to have been introduced into this country through New Orleans where, due to its similarity to the French game of *poque,* it acquired that name. Southern gentlemen who played the game but were untutored in French pronunciation gave it two syllables—"pok-uh"—which is very similar to their pronunciation of "poker." Northerners who learned the game from these gentlemen quite obviously deduced, therefore, that it was spelled the same.

Pop Goes the Weasel. *Where do we get the expression "Pop goes the Weasel"?*

When you sing:

> "That's the way the money goes;
> Pop goes the weasel . . ."

you're referring to the opening and shutting of a pocketbook. "Weasel" or "weaselskin" was a popular slang name for a "pocketbook" when the verse was written.

Pope. *How did the "Pope" get that name?*

This term comes from the Italian *papa,* meaning, of course, "father."

192

Porcelain. *Why is chinaware called "porcelain"?*

The word is from the French *porcelaine*—and literally means "like a pig." The back of cowrie shells looks something like a pig's back and so these little shells were named "little pig" shells. Chinese earthenware has a white glossy look like the inside of these shells—and so it too was given this name.

Pork Barrel. *How did we come to call plunder by politicians "dipping into the pork barrel"?*

It was once the custom in country stores to keep available an open barrel of salt pork. Certain persons of the community would, at times, dip into the pork barrel—just as they dipped into the cracker barrel—and help themselves. And so we came to use the term "pork barrel" to indicate a common fund of money into which our legislators dip for their own and their constituents' more personal projects.

Port. *What is the reason we call the larboard or "left" side of a vessel the "port" side?*

The steering oar of ancient sailing vessels was on the right side. The opposite, or left side, was therefore the one laid up against the dock for unloading. This side was nearest the "port"; and, if necessary, it had in it a cargo "port" or opening. Both terms come from the same Latin root *port-*, meaning "opening." The change from calling this side of the vessel "larboard" was brought about by the confusion often arising out of the similarity of sound between "larboard" and "starboard."

Porterhouse Steak. *Who was the Porter for whom the "porterhouse steak" was named?*

An early New York tavern keeper. The "Porter House" was famous for its steaks but on one occasion ran out of them. So Porter dipped into his larder and took out a large piece of sirloin he'd been keeping for roasting. He cut a piece and broiled it. The steak was found to be delicious and was added to the bill of fare as "porter-house" steak.

Posthaste. *Why do we use "posthaste" to mean as fast as possible?*

Because back in the days when all travel was by horse, traveling by post—that is, by public coach—was faster than traveling by private carriage. The owner of a private vehicle had to stop to rest his horses, but "post horses" were used in relays and the coach kept rolling.

Potluck. *What is the reason an impromptu meal is called "potluck"?*

It was once customary for the housewife to have a pot on the fire into which all scraps of meat and vegetables were thrown. She "kept the pot boiling" and there was always stew available—but what it tasted like was a matter of "potluck."

Potter's Field. *Where did we get the name "potter's field" for a piece of ground used as a burial place for the poor?*

It comes from the Bible (Matthew 27:6-7). After Judas had hanged himself for betraying the Saviour for thirty pieces of silver, the chief priests picked up the silver which he had cast down. They said, " 'It is not lawful

194

for to put them into the treasury, because it is the price of blood.' And they took counsel, ānd bought with them the potter's field, to bury strangers in."

Pound Cake. *How did "pound cake" come to be called by that name?*

It's because in old recipes for the cake many of the principal ingredients were listed as a "pound" of this and a "pound" of that.

Powwow. *Why do we call a council a "powwow"?*

"Powwow" is an Indian word. The Indians of the New England coast first used it in referring to their medicine man; then it was transferred to their ceremonial rites; afterwards, it came to mean any gathering at all.

Prestige. *What is the origin of the word "prestige"?*

It comes directly from the Latin *praestigium,* meaning a "delusion" or "illusion." The plural of this Latin word, however, means "jugglers' tricks." But there is a Latin term that more nearly approximates our concept of "prestige"—*praestringere oculos;* this means "to blindfold" and, by analogy, to "dazzle the eyes."

Printer's Devil. *How did a printer's assistant come to be called a "printer's devil"?*

The apprentice boys of early print shops so often had their faces begrimed with ink that they looked as black as any devil employed to stoke the furnaces of Hell—and so they were called "devils." The story is told that when Aldus Manutius, the sixteenth century Venetian printer, employed a Negro boy as a helper, the good people of the city became convinced the boy was an imp from Hell. Accusations were made against Aldus and in defense he was forced to publish this notice: "I, Aldus Manutius, printer to the Holy Church and to the Doge, have this day made public exposure of my 'devil.' All who think he is not flesh and blood may come and pinch him."

Private Soldier. *Why do we call a common soldier a "private" soldier?*

Because in the early days in England the men who entered government service in any executive capacity—including those who became officers in the army—were said to have entered "public life." Others were called "private citizens." The common soldier was a private citizen who enlisted or was drafted into service. Since it was presumed that he had not adopted soldiering as a career, he was called a "private soldier" as opposed to a "public officer." In time, however, "public" was dropped from in front of the word "officer" and "soldier" from after the word "private."

Prize Ring. *How did the spot where two prize fighters meet come to be called a "ring" when it's square?*

The reason is to be found in the history of the rules of the sport. Figg, the first recognized boxing champion of England, adopted his own set of rules. These called for a square of eight feet drawn in the center of the stage. Within this square the rival fighters "toed the mark," as it was then termed, or "squared off" to begin hostilities. Later, Broughton's rules were adopted. They called for

196

a square, a yard across, drawn in the middle of the stage. "For every set-to," the rules said, "the rival seconds must bring their men to opposite sides of the square from where the fighting should begin." Still later, when the contestants were first made to keep the fight within a square enclosure, the rules said: "There should be drawn in that square a circle five feet in diameter, known as the center, where contestants shall meet for the beginning of each round." It is this "ring" that has given its name to the enclosure in which the boxers meet.

Proletariat. *Where does the term "proletariat" come from?*

From the Latin *proletarius*—the name given by the ancient Romans to the lowest class in the community. "This class," the historians of that time said, "contributes nothing to the state but offspring."

Prude. *Why do we call a prissy person a "prude"?*

Because the French think of a proud woman as being discreet. The French use the word *prudefemme*—which literally means "proud woman"—to denote a discreet woman and we took our "prude" from this word—adding the thought of being overly discreet.

Pull One's Leg. *What is the reason we say that one person joshing another is "pulling his leg"?*

The allusion is to tripping up a man by catching at his foot or "pulling his leg." This, of course, makes the man fall—and to see a person fall is considered comic by all mankind.

Pull Up Socks; Pull Up Stakes. *Is there any connection between a man who "pulls up his socks" and one who "pulls up stakes"?*

None whatsoever. The phrase "pull up his socks" means to "buck up" and is an allusion to the man about to call upon a business prospect who spruces up his appearance —and as the final touch, "pulls up his socks." The expression "pull up stakes" is an allusion to the camper who "pulls up" the tent pegs or "stakes" as he strikes his tent.

Pumpernickel. *Why is "pumpernickel" bread called that?*

This name for a special type of bread is German and in German "nickel" is a common abbreviation of the personal name "Nicolaus," while "pumper" means "the noise of a heavy fall." For some strange reason these two words, when combined, came to mean "a coarse, dark-complexioned, brutish fellow"—and "pumpernickel" bread is both coarse and dark.

Pup Tent. *How did the "pup tent" get that name?*

These tents are smaller than other tents and were named by the Union soldiers in the Civil War. When they were introduced and the soldiers were told to use them, they appeared so much like dog kennels to the men that one of them stuck his head out and began to bark. The idea took hold and soon the whole camp was barking. The tents were therefore called "dog tents"—the name soon degenerating into "pup tents."

Puppy. *Where does the word "puppy" come from?*

From the French *poupée*, meaning "doll." By extension, it means any sort of a plaything—including a young dog.

198

Purchase. *How did the word "purchase" gets its present meaning?*

"Purchase" comes from the French *pourchasser* which means "to hunt." Once upon a time stores had no show windows and would-be purchasers had to "hunt" for what they wanted—though they were helped somewhat by apprentices who stood outside the stores and asked what they wanted as they passed by.

Put on Side. *What is the reason we say a pretentious person "puts on side"?*

A "side coat" is a long, trailing coat—from the Anglo-Saxon *sid* meaning "great," "wide," or "long." And "putting on side" is to dress in a "side coat" or other long clothing and act the superior person.

Pyrrhic Victory. *Why do we call a success gained at too great cost a "Pyrrhic victory"?*

This name for a ruinous victory is an allusion to the victories of King Pyrrhus of Epirus over the Romans about 280 B.C. With a force of 25,000 men, Pyrrhus met the Romans under the Consul Laevinius at Heraclea—the first time that Greeks and Romans had engaged each other in battle on such a large scale. In the end, because of his cavalry and elephants, Pyrrhus severely defeated the Romans—but not until both sides had suffered extremely heavy losses. Rome refused to make peace with the victor and the following year Pyrrhus again defeated the Romans at Asculum—in two engagements in which he lost most of his army. According to Plutarch, when Pyrrhus was congratulated on the victory he said, "Such another victory and we are utterly undone."

QUIZ 7

(Answers on page 278)

1. Why do we say a person who is "laying low" is "playing possum"?
2. What is the origin of the expression "a nose for news"?
3. Why is a book written for popular consumption called a "potboiler"?
4. Where did a small amount of money put aside by a woman get the name "egg money"?
5. Why do we use "on the dot" to mean "on time"?
6. What is the reason a simple person is called a "ninny"?
7. Why is a pugilist called a "pug"?
8. What is the origin of the expression, "put that in your pipe and smoke it"?
9. Why do we say a person who is all dressed up is "dressed fit to kill"?
10. How did a "penknife" come to be called that?
11. Why is something that increases in size rapidly said to "snowball"?
12. What is the reason an alto horn is called a "peck horn"?
13. Where did we get the term "party," meaning a person?
14. What is the origin of the expression "get it in the neck"?
15. Why do we say a foolish person is "nutty"?
16. Where does the word "pandemonium" come from?
17. What is the origin of the term "picnic"?
18. Why do we call a woman inclined to malicious gossip a "cat" or "catty"?
19. Why is a man's room in the house called his "den"?
20. What is the reason a machine for processing cotton is called a cotton "gin"?

Quack. *Why is a medical charlatan pretending to be a physician called a "quack"?*

Because he boasts of his salves. "Quack" is really an abbreviation of "quacksalver," which comes from the Dutch *kwakzalver*—and this has this idea of "quacking about one's salves." But the idea behind all these terms is that the "quack" is like the duck—he makes a big noise over nothing.

Quaker. *How did the "Quakers" get that name?*

George Fox, the founder of the Society of Friends, in his speeches admonished the magistrates of England and told them they should "quake" at the word of the Lord. The term "Quakers" comes from this phrase—and was devised by Justice Bennet, a magistrate of Derby.

Quarantine. *Where does the word "quarantine" come from?*

From the Italian *quaranta*, meaning "forty." In early days, a ship suspected of being infected with some contagious disease was kept outside of port for forty days—in "quarantine."

Quarter. *Why do we say we give "no quarter" when we mean we show "no mercy"?*

Because originally to "give quarter" meant to send conquered enemy soldiers to a special section or "quarter" where they remained until their fate was determined. They could be set free, ransomed, or enslaved. If they were killed instead they were given "no quarter."

Queer Card. *What is the reason a queer person is called a "queer card"?*

In a game of bridge, whist, or the like, if your partner makes an unusual lead, the card played is a "queer" card —and he's a "queer card" for having led it. A person is called a "card" by a shortening of the term.

Quibble. *Why do we call a petty argument over a minor point "quibbling"?*

The word comes from the Latin *quibus*. This is the dative and the ablative of *qui,* meaning "who" or "which"—and it was used so much in legal documents and fought over to such an extent by lawyers that it gave us the term "quibble."

Quinsy. *How did the disease "quinsy" get that name?*

The word comes from the Greek *kynanche.* This means both "sore throat" and "dog collar"—because a dog collar produces a choking effect. People suffering with acute "quinsy" often find it difficult to open their mouths and so have a feeling of choking.

202

Quintessence. *Why do we call the ultimate essence the "quintessence"?*

Because the ancient Greeks believed there were forms in which matter could exist—fire, air, water, and earth. But the Pythagorean philosophers added a fifth form—ether. It was more subtle than the others and was considered the purest. This was the fifth essence; the Latin word *quintus* means "fifth."

Quiz. *How did "quiz" come into the English language?*

Because of a bet. A man named Daly, who was manager of the Dublin Theater, made a bet that he would introduce into the English language within twenty-four hours a new word that had no meaning. Accordingly, on every wall in Dublin and every other place accessible, Daly had chalked up the four mystic letters Q-U-I-Z. That day all Dublin was inquiring what they meant, the people saying to each other: "Quiz? Quiz? What does it mean?" Daly won his bet—and the word has remained in our language to this day. It is quite probable, however, that his choice of letters—or at least, the continued popularity of the term—was influenced by the similarity in sound and meaning to the word "inquisition."

```
R R R R R R
R           R
R    R      R
R           R
R R R R R R
```

Rabbit Punch. *Why do we call a punch behind the ear in boxing a "rabbit punch"?*

Because at one time a poacher catching a rabbit in a snare which in itself had not killed the animal would kill it with a blow on the back of the neck.

Rack One's Brains. *What is the reason a person who is struggling to remember something is said to "rack his brains"?*

As used here, "rack" means "to stretch or strain by force"—as a person is stretched on the "rack" or wheel—and that is a rather vivid metaphorical description of the process of remembering.

Radar. *How did "radar" get its name?*

It's just a combination of the initial letters of "radio direction and ranging"—an exact description of what it does.

Radio. *Where did "radio" get that name?*

The word is derived from the Latin *radius,* meaning a "staff," or the "spoke of a wheel," or a "ray of light." Radio waves travel like rays of light—going out in all directions like the spokes of a wheel.

204

Ragtime. *How did we come to call syncopated music "ragtime"?*

The term "ragtime" originally meant "haphazard, careless, and happy-go-lucky." It was applied to an army under loose discipline—as opposed to one that was made to keep step. "Ragtime" music is equally happy-go-lucky and careless of the music as written.

Raining Cats and Dogs. *What is the origin of the expression "raining cats and dogs"?*

It comes from Norse mythology—in which the cat symbolizes heavy rain, while the dog, an attendant of Odin, the storm god, represents great blasts of wind. The proverbial enmity of cats and dogs must have led to the choice of these animals to represent the conflict of the elements in a storm—just as it has increased the popularity of the expression.

Rap. *Why do we say that something that's practically worthless is "not worth a rap"?*

Because there was a great scarcity of small coins in Ireland in the 1700's—and so a counterfeit halfpenny which was introduced gained wide circulation. This coin was called a "rap"—and it was worth no more than a quarter of its face value.

Real Estate. *Where did land get the name "real estate"?*

From England—where the term originally meant a "royal grant." All land once belonged to the king in England, and the only way a person could get any of it was by royal grant.

Red Cent. *What is the reason we add the word "red" in the phrase "not a red cent"?*

As white is the color of tin or silver and black is the color of iron, so "red" is the color of copper—and the "cent" is made of copper.

Red Herring. *How did we come to call misdirection "drawing a red herring across the trail"?*

This term for an attempt to distract attention from the main issue comes from fox hunting. A red herring has a very strong odor—because of the way it's cured. And so, hounds set on the scent of a fox may be distracted by the smell of a red herring dragged across the trail. Then the hounds will follow the trail of the red herring instead of the fox.

Red-Letter Day. *Why do we call an important day in our lives a "red letter day"?*

In the early prayer books, the Saints' days and church festivals were printed in red ink. Some prayer books are still printed in this style and many calendars today have the Sundays and holidays indicated by red letters or figures. So, a "red-letter day," since it's a holiday, is one that we look forward to with pleasure or look back upon with joy.

Red Tape. *Where did governmental delay get the name "red tape"?*

From England—where for centuries the British government has followed the custom of tying up official papers with red tape. The everlasting tying and untying of the

206

red tape which bound the dispatch and document cases led men to pick it as the symbol of useless delay. The present British "red tape" is pink.

Return to Our Muttons. *What is the origin of the expression "let us return to our muttons"?*

The phrase means "Let us return to the subject matter from which we have wandered" and it comes from an old French play, "L'Avocat Patelin," by Blanchet. In the play Guillaume, a draper, was robbed by Patelin, a lawyer, of six ells of cloth and by Agnelet, his shepherd, of twenty-six sheep. He brought suit against his shepherd and found that the man was defended by Patelin. He confused the two losses and the judge said, *"Revenons à nos moutons"*—meaning "Let us return to our sheep." The phrase caught on and spread from France to England in only partial translation.

Rhyme or Reason. *Why do we say "without rhyme or reason"?*

Some poems have no sense to them but at least have "rhyme"; some prose is awkward but at least has "reason."

Ride and Tie. *How did a slow pace come to be called progress by "ride and tie"?*

Because this is a common method of travel in the Southwest where two persons with only one horse will both ride it. As they start out on a journey, one "rides" ahead a little way, "ties" the horse to a tree, and continues on foot. The second comes up to the horse, mounts, passes the first and then dismounts and ties the horse to a post so that the first person can repeat the process.

207

Right and Left. *Why do we refer to a conservative political party as a "party of the Right" and a liberal party as a "party of the Left"?*

Because that's how they're traditionally seated in the legislatures of Europe. The presiding officer was generally a man of position, and therefore a conservative. So he seated the conservatives on his right, to honor them more than the liberals he seated on his left.

Right Foot Foremost. *Where did we get the expression "right foot foremost"?*

From ancient Rome—where it was once believed that bad luck was brought to a house by a person who crossed the threshold with his left foot. This belief was so strong that a boy was often stationed at the door to make sure all visitors entered the house "right foot foremost."

Right Off the Reel. *How did we come to say a person with ready answers gives them "right off the reel"?*

The original meaning of this phrase was "without intermission" rather than "without hesitation," and the allusion is to a rope or thread being unwound—off the reel.

Ring the Bell. *Why do we say a success "rings the bell"?*

At county fairs there's a strength-testing machine which is operated by hitting a block with a sledge. This operates an arm of wood which sends a weight up a wire. If you hit the block hard enough the weight will go to the top of the device and ring a bell. The usual prize for this achievement is a cigar. Similarly, if you hit the bull's eye at a shooting gallery you ring a bell.

208

Ringleader. *What is the reason the leader of a group of people is called a "ringleader"?*

The term comes from dancing. Many old dances began with all the participants holding hands in a ring. Then the circle was broken and one person led the rest of the "ring" through the figures of the dance.

Rise. *Why do we say we "get a rise" out of a person when he shows he can't take a joke?*

The expression comes from angling. If you place the right lure in the right spot at the right time, the fish will "rise" to the bait—and be caught.

Rival. *What is the derivation of the word "rival"?*

It comes from the Latin word for "stream"—*rivus*. The original "rivals" were people who lived on opposite sides of a stream and fought bitterly over which side of the stream was the better to live on. Many such communities still do.

Rob Peter to Pay Paul. *Where did we get the expression "rob Peter to pay Paul"?*

Originally from the supposed rivalry between St. Peter, who was the Apostle to the Jews, and St. Paul, who was the Apostle to the Gentiles. But the expression has undoubtedly survived because of the alliteration.

Robin Hood's Barn. *Why do we say a person who arrives at a decision in a roundabout way goes "around Robin Hood's barn"?*

Because he goes the longest way round. Robin Hood considered all of Sherwood Forest his home, all of it his barn—in popular imagination, there could be no larger.

Roland for Your Oliver. *Where did we get the expression "a Roland for your Oliver"?*

From an incident in French history. Roland and Oliver were two of Charlemagne's paladins who, the story goes, fought for five days without either gaining the advantage over the other because they were so evenly matched. So the phrase means to give "blow for blow."

Rope Them In. *Why do we say a successful attraction "ropes them in"?*

The term is an allusion to the once common practice of drawing in hay with a rope. After the hay had been heaped in windrows, a rope with a horse attached to each end was swept like a net around the row, bringing the hay together into a stack.

Round Robin. *What is the reason a petition signed by a number of people is called a "round robin"?*

It's because such petitions were originally signed in a circle so that no single name headed the list. The term is a corruption of the French *rond*, meaning "round," and *ruban*, meaning a "ribbon"—the circle of signatures creating the impression of a "round ribbon."

Royal Road to Learning. *Where did we get the expression "the royal road to learning"?*

From the legend of 2,200 years ago that the King of Egypt asked Euclid if there wasn't an easy way for him to learn geometry. To this, Euclid replied: "Sire, there is no royal road to learning."

Rubicon. *Why does the expression "crossing the Rubicon" mean no turning back?*

Because when Caesar crossed the Rubicon River in 49 B.C. with his army—going from his own province of Gaul into Italy contrary to the prohibition of the civil government in Rome—he was, in effect, declaring war and there was no turning back.

Rule of Thumb. *How did rough measurements come to be called "by rule of thumb"?*

Because that's one way to make rough measurements. The first joint of the thumb is approximately one inch long. A "foot" was once the length of a foot; a "hand," the width of a hand; an "ell," the length of the arms from elbow to elbow; and a "fathom," the length of the arms outstretched. We still use a "finger" to measure drinks.

Rumble Seat. *Why is a "rumble seat" so called?*

The term was first applied to the seat behind the body of the carriage which was provided for servants. It got its name from the fact that when sitting in it you could hear the "rumble" of the carriage as it rolled over the road.

Runcible Spoon. *How did the "runcible spoon" get that name?*

A "runcible spoon" is a tined spoon with a cutting edge —and it was named in jocose allusion to the battle of "Rancevaux," which was more a slaughter than a battle.

S S S S S S S
S   S
S   S   S
S   S
S S S S S S S

Sabotage. *Where does the word "sabotage" come from?*

The word—which originally meant a wilful destruction of machinery by workmen in industrial disputes—is French and is derived from *sabot*, the name of the French workmen's wooden shoe. When looms were first introduced in France the workmen of the mills objected to them and threw their wooden shoes into the looms in order to put them out-of-order.

Sack. *How did the expression "get the sack" come to mean "discharged"?*

In the days when most artisans and mechanics lived on the job they brought their tools to work with them in a "sack"; and then left the tools and sack with their employer for safekeeping. When the mechanic was discharged his employer gave him back his sack of tools—he literally "got the sack."

Sail Close to the Wind. *Why do we say a person who is following a course that is close to being illegal is "sailing close to the wind"?*

Because a sailing vessel "sailing close to the wind" is in danger of being caught by a gust and jibing or keeling over—and so being swamped. So too, a person engaging in a practice that is just short of being illegal is in danger of being caught.

Salad Days. *What is the reason we call a man's youth his "salad days"?*

It's because when a man is young, he's "green"—and "greens" go into making a "salad."

Salary. *Where did we get the word "salary"?*

From the ancient Romans. The word literally means "salt money." The Roman soldier was once given an allowance of salt; then he was given an allowance of money for the purchase of salt. This was called a *salarium*—from *sal*, meaning "salt."

Sally Lunn. *How did "Sally Lunn" cakes get that name?*

They were named for a pastry cook of Bath, England. The original "Sally Lunn" lived in the late eighteenth century and cried her wares on the street. They became famous and so perpetuated her name.

Salt. *Why do we say a questionable statement should be "taken with a grain of salt"?*

Because salt added to food brings out the flavor. If you are presented with something and "swallow it whole" you may not notice any taint—but if you take it "with a grain of salt" the salt will accentuate the flavor and enable you to test its worth.

Salt-Water Taffy. *What is the reason we call the taffy candy "salt-water taffy"?*

This taffy is so labeled by the manufacturer because we have all come to associate it with the little stands that sell it along the boardwalks of salt-water resorts. But, according to an old legend, even this association was accidental. In 1818, so this story goes, a small candy store situated on the boardwalk in Atlantic City, New Jersey, was damaged in the middle of the summer by a heavy storm. After the storm was over, the proprietor came back to his stand to discover that water from the ocean had splashed over all the taffy in his case. So he put up a sign "Salt-water taffy—10 cents." The name caught the fancy of the public and has been used ever since.

Sam Patch. *Where did we get the expression "like Sam Patch" as a synonym for "quick and reckless"?*
It's an illusion to a famous jumper and daredevil named Sam Patch. His most famous feat was a jump, on November 6, 1829, down the Falls at Rochester, New York.

Sandwich. *Who named the "sandwich" that?*
The mid-eighteenth century John Montague, Fourth Earl of "Sandwich." Montague loved to play cards so much that he never wanted to take time out to eat. So he solved the problem by placing slices of beef between two pieces of bread and munching away while he played.

Sands Are Running Out. *Why do we say "the sands are running out" when we mean that time is getting short?*
Because at one time a sand-clock was used to tell the passing of time. It was composed of two compartments of glass and the sand was spilled from one to the other. When one section was almost emptied of its sand you knew that time was almost up.

214

Santa Claus. *How did "Santa Claus" get his name?*
The term comes from the Dutch dialect name for St. Nicholas—*Sint Klass*. St. Nicholas is the patron saint of children and in Holland gifts were once given to children in his name and on his day, which is shortly before Christmas. In time this custom was transferred to Christmas and expanded to include gifts for all. St. Nicholas is also the patron saint of scholars, travelers, sailors, and pawnbrokers.

Sarcophagus. *Where do we get the word "sarcophagus"?*
"Sarcophagus" was originally the name of the stone chosen by the ancients for their coffins—and not for the coffins themselves. The stone was believed to consume the body placed within it and the name comes from this belief—being a combination of the Greek *sarx*, meaning "flesh," and *phagein*, meaning "to eat."

Sardonic Laughter. *How did mocking laughter come to be called "sardonic"?*
It's because *Herba Sardonia*—which grows in Sardinia—is a poison so bitter to the taste that it causes the nerves to twitch and a painful smile to appear on the face of the eater.

Scapegoat. *Why is a person who suffers for another's deeds called a "scapegoat"?*
The Book of Leviticus in the Bible tells how on the Day of Atonement the sins of the people were symbolically placed upon the head of a goat and the "goat" was then allowed to "escape" into the wilderness. Thus the term "scapegoat" literally means "escaping goat."

215

School. *What is the origin of the word "school"?*

The word is from the Greek and originally meant "leisure." In ancient Greece only a person with leisure could "go to school."

Scoop. *Where did newspapermen get the word "scoop," as a synonym for "news-beat"?*

The use of this term by newspapermen comes from poker. If there's a big pot and you are the winner, you "scoop" up the chips. From this we get the meaning of "winning over others in large measure"—which is what a paper does when it gets a "scoop."

Scot-Free. *Does the "scot" of "scot-free" come from Scotland?*

No. The "scot" of the term comes from the Anglo-Saxon *sceot*, meaning "money put into a general fund" —hence, a "tax." The "scot" was the original "income tax"—since it was levied upon the people according to their ability to pay. "Scot-free" first meant "tax free."

Seventh Heaven. *Why do we say we're in "seventh heaven" when we're as happy as we can be?*

Because the Mohammedans believe there are seven heavens piled one upon the other and that each heaven represents greater happiness than the previous one. God himself and the angels are all located in the seventh or topmost heaven.

Shanghai. *What is the reason we use the word "shanghai" to mean kidnapping a man for a ship's crew?*

It's because British sailors so treated were likely to find themselves shipped out on a long voyage to a distant port

216

—and since Shanghai was on the other side of the world they used the name of this port to represent any distant place.

Shanty. *How did "shanty" come to mean a tumble-down house?*

It started in Canada; *chantier* was the name the early French settlers gave to the hut in the forest which served as their headquarters. Here they slept and stored their tools. "Shanty" is a corruption of *"chantier."*

Shavetail. *What is the reason a second lieutenant in the army is called a "shavetail"?*

This not very complimentary name comes from the similarity in strangeness, antics and lack of steadiness between new young officers and new young mules purchased by the government. When these mules are purchased, their tails are close-shaven and appear almost as hairless as the upper lips of very young men.

Shebang. *Where did we get the expression "the whole shebang"?*

It comes from an Irish name for a speakeasy—that is, a drinking place without a license—*shebeen.* A truculent Irishman deep in drink would offer to take on every one present—"the whole shebeen."

Sheriff. *How did a "sheriff" get that name?*

The term is derived from the Anglo-Saxon title—*shire reeve.* The *shire reeve* of eleventh century England was an official appointed by the king to administer the local government, enforce the law, and collect the king's taxes.

217

Shillelagh. *Why do the Irish call a club a "shillelagh"?*

The true Irish "shillelagh" is made of oak—and is named for the town of Shillelagh in County Wicklow, Ireland which is celebrated for its fine oak trees.

Shilly-Shally. *What is the reason we say a person who can't make up his mind is "shilly-shallying"?*

The person who can't make up his mind constantly asks himself questions; and the term is a corruption of "Shill I? Shall I?"—"shill" being a weak form of "shall."

Shimmy. *Why do we call a wiggly dance a "shimmy"?*

The dance got its name from an article of clothing—the "chemise." When you dance the "shimmy" you wiggle your hips and shoulders pretty much as you would when getting into a chemise. *Chemise* is the French word for "shirt."

Shindig. *How did a party come to be called a "shindig"?*

If the party gets rough enough, the men begin to fight and "dig" each other in the "shins" with the toe of their boots. "Shindig" was first used in reference to this blow; then to the party itself—though only a rough one—and finally to any party at all.

Shinplaster. *Why are bank notes for less than a dollar called "shinplaster"?*

Because the small bank notes of the Revolutionary War period were practically worthless—except perhaps for use as a "plaster" on a wound in the leg or wrapped about the "shins" to ward off the cold breezes.

218

Shirt Off One's Back. *What is the reason we say a really generous person will "give you the shirt off his back"?*
Because this once represented the ultimate in generosity. In the days when men wore only three pieces of wearing apparel—coat, pants, and shirt—a person could give you his coat and still remain fully covered. But if he then "gave you the shirt off his back," that was all he could give—within the limits of decency.

Shoddy. *How did near-worthless material come to be called "shoddy"?*
In the process of weaving cloth, a certain amount of fluff is thrown off. This was called "shoddy" from the dialect verb *shode*, meaning "shedding" or "separating." The fluff was then used in making new wool—but, because it was short-stapled, clothes made from it did not last long.

Shoestring. *Why do we say of a man who has built his business up from next-to-nothing, "he started on a shoe-string"?*
The allusion is to a street peddler who offers shoestrings for sale. This form of business endeavor requires no office, no tools, and less capital than almost any other type imaginable.

Shrimp. *Is there a connection between "shrimp" as a nickname for a small person and the sea food?*
There is none. The "shrimp" that's applied to a small person comes from the Anglo-Saxon *scrine-an*, meaning "to shrink"; it's used humorously to indicate the idea that the person is so small he must have "shrunk" to achieve his size.

Shucks. *Why do we say "oh, shucks" and "he's not worth shucks"?*

In both expressions "shucks" is used to indicate worthlessness. The "shucks" referred to are corn shucks—for at one time the husks of corn were considered worthless.

Siamese Twins. *What is the reason twins that are joined together by flesh or bone are called "Siamese twins"?*

It's because the first of these twins to be widely exhibited —Chang and Eng—were born in Siam. These twins— who were joined at the waist—eventually settled down as farmers in North Carolina and married two sisters. Chang had six children and Eng five.

Sign Off. *How did a complete termination come to be called a "sign off"?*

The reference is to receipting a bill or other commercial paper. If a creditor agrees to accept a debtor's offer to pay a part for the whole, he concludes the transaction by signing the bill, "Paid." The account is no longer open; it has been "signed off" the books.

Silhouette. *Where did we get the word "silhouette"?*

The term is derived from the name of the French Comptroller General in 1759, Etienne de Silhouette, who became famous for his economy measures. Under Silhouette business and commerce were stripped of unnecessary detail—even paintings were reduced to mere outlines. In this spirit of economy, portraits in black-and-white outline became popular—and were named "silhouettes" in honor of the financier whose economy had suggested them.

Silver Hook. *What is the origin of the expression "to angle with a silver hook"?*

The "silver hook" is money—a bribe. If you've failed to catch fish by the usual means and have gone to market and bought some instead—well, then you've "angled with a silver hook."

Silver Spoon. *Why do we say a son of the rich is "born with a silver spoon in his mouth"?*

Because it was once the custom for the godparents of a child to present it with a silver spoon at the christening. But a child born of wealthy parents did not have to wait until his christening to sup from silver—he was practically "born with a silver spoon in his mouth."

Simony. *How did bribery come to be called "simony"?*

The term was first used in old English law to refer to the act of procuring an appointment to an important church position in return for a bribe. This practice got its name from Simon Magus who offered money to the Apostles Peter and John in the hope of obtaining a position of prominence like theirs.

Sit Above the Salt. *What is the reason we say a person of prominence "sits above the salt"?*

The expression originally meant to be placed at the table as an honored guest—at least equal in rank to the lord of the manor. For in Saxon times in England, the saltcellar was set as a dividing line at the table—to separate the persons who used the salt as guests of the host from the men of the household who worked for him and so earned the right to share the salt.

Sit On One's Hands. *Where did we get the expression "sitting on his hands" to describe an unresponsive person?*

From the theatre—where, if the audience "sits on its hands," it obviously cannot applaud.

Skid On; Skids Under. *Is there any connection between the phrases "put the skid on" and "put the skids under"?*

Only through the use of the word "skid." To "put the skid on" means "to slow up"—and the allusion is to putting a "skid block" or "skid chain" on the wheel of a wagon. To "put the skids under" is to "speed-up"—and the allusion is to the skids used by loggers in getting the logs into the water. To "grease the skids" refers to another type of skid—that placed beneath a vessel to launch it. These skids are coated with grease or ripe bananas so that the ship will slip easily into the water.

Skin of His Teeth. *Why do we say a person gets by "by the skin of his teeth"?*

The expression is a literal translation from the Hebrew text of the Book of Job. Since a person's teeth have no skin, for him to get by "by the skin of his teeth" is to get by with no margin at all.

Skinflint. *What is the reason we call a parsimonious person a "skinflint"?*

Bits of flint were once used to make fire. The rocks could be split into smaller and smaller pieces and each piece could be used for this purpose. A "skinflint" was once one who, in trying to save a penny on flint, would split a piece down to its final layer or "skin."

Skullduggery. *How did evil actions come to be called "skullduggery"?*

Grave robbing was once a common crime and a grave robber was called a "skull digger." From this, any criminal activity—especially one practiced at night—came to be called "skulldigging" or "skullduggery."

Skunked. *Why do we say that a badly beaten person is "skunked"?*

The person who is defeated in a game so thoroughly that he has failed to score feels, not only that he has been humiliated, but that it was a "skunk" that did it.

Skylark. *Where did we get the term "skylark"?*

"Lark" is derived from the Anglo-Saxon *lac* which means "play" or "fun." "Skylarking" comes from the sailors' custom of mounting the highest yards of sailing vessels—known as "skyscrapers"—and then sliding down.

Slapstick. *Why is rough, raucous comedy called "slapstick" comedy?*

It is named for a device used by low comedians on the stage. Two pieces of wood are fastened together loosely so that when wielded as a club they produce a loud *whack!* To produce laughter the comedians spank each other with this device, which they call a "slapstick."

Slick as a Whistle. *What is the reason we use the word "whistle" in the expression "slick as a whistle"?*

It's because it is "slick"—that is, "sleek"—inside. Wind blown into a reed pipe is slowed up by the reed but a whistle has no obstruction at all.

Slide, Kelly, Slide. *Where did we get the expression "slide, Kelly, slide"?*

In the late 1880's and early '90's there was a great baseball hero, Mike "King" Kelly, who excelled in stealing bases. The fans were all for him and when King Kelly lit out to steal a base, they would all encourage him by shouting, "Slide, Kelly, Slide."

Slush Fund. *How did a "slush fund" get that name?*

Aboard a sailing ship "slush" is waste fat from the galley used to grease the masts. All extra slush used to be the cook's perquisite—and he didn't have to account for the money he made from selling it. Likewise, a "slush fund" is money that need not be accounted for—and often had better not be.

Sneeze At. *Why do we say something worthwhile is "not to be sneezed at"?*

If a statement seems worthless, you may not bother to reply; you may merely make the sound of a sneeze—"humph," as we try to write it. Something worthwhile, however, is "not to be sneezed at."

Snob. *What is the origin of the term "snob"?*

The word comes from the Scottish *snab*, meaning "boy" or "servant." College students in England were at one time all members of the nobility—and applied *snab* in the sense of "servant" to the townsmen. The word "*snab*" was changed to "snob" in the 1600's when Cambridge University decided to admit commoners as students. Cambridge required that such students, when registering, describe their social position with the Latin words *Sine*

Nobilitate, meaning "without nobility." The students abbreviated this to *S. Nob.* When spoken, this abbreviation seemed so much like the word *"snab"* it came to be written "snob" and used to signify "a pretender to position."

Sockdolager. *Where did we get the word "sockdolager"?*
The term was originally one applied to a ranting revivalist. It's just an inverted form of "doxologer." Soon, however, "sockdolager" came to be applied to a knockout blow in boxing—because of the way it sounds.

Soft Soap. *What is the origin of the expression "soft soap"?*
The term was first used as a synonym for "flattery" by confidence men. Since soap that has become soft is extremely slippery, you used "soft soap" to "grease the skids" you put under a "sucker."

Soldier. *How did the "soldier" get his name?*
The word comes from the Latin *solidus*—the name of a gold coin. The Roman "soldier" worked for whichever master paid him; he was a mercenary.

Solon. *Why do we call a member of Congress a "Solon"?*
This name for a member of Congress had its origin in Greek history. Solon was an Athenian noted for his learning and wisdom. He was also entrusted with the task of revising the Athenian Constitution. Probably more for this second reason than for the first, members of the United States Congress are called "Solons."

Son-of-a-Gun. *Where did we get the expression "son-of-a-gun"?*

From British sea slang. At one time the sailors in the British Navy were allowed to take their wives with them on long sea voyages. A child born to a sailor's wife at sea was called a "son-of-a-gun"—because it was literally born beneath the "guns" of a ship. At a later date the term was extended to include those conceived aboard the ship—and not always by a wife.

Sound as a Bell. *How did we come to say this or that is as "sound as a bell"?*

A pun is intended. If a bell is cracked, it won't ring; if it won't ring, it won't "sound"; if it won't sound, it's not "sound."

Sour Grapes. *What is the origin of the term "sour grapes"?*

The allusion is to the fable of the fox who tried to reach some grapes hanging up on a vine. When he was finally convinced that he could not get them, he turned away and said, "Well, they're 'sour' anyway."

Southpaw. *Why do we call a left-handed person a "south-paw"?*

All major league baseball diamonds are laid out so that the batter will face east, thus putting the afternoon sun behind his back and making it easier for him to see the ball. Therefore, when the pitcher faces the batter he's facing west and his left arm is to the south. So, if he pitches left-handed, he's pitching with his "south paw."

226

Sparking. *What is the reason love-making is called "sparking"?*

It's because kissing can produce a tingle that's not unlike that produced by a static electric "spark."

Spars. *How did the "Spars" get their name?*

This name for the women members of the United States Coast Guard comes from the Coast Guard's Latin motto, *Semper Paratus,* meaning "Always Ready." The "S" is from the first word; the "PAR" is from the second.

Spats. *Why are cloth ankle protectors called "spats"?*

These ankle protectors were originally called "spatter-dashers"—the "dash" being used in the same sense as in the "dashboard" of a carriage—and they were originally used to protect the ankle against mud, rather than cold.

Speakeasy. *Where did we get "speakeasy" as the name for an illicit saloon?*

The term is Irish in origin. You couldn't raise your voice riotously or kick up a rumpus in an establishment where liquor was sold contrary to the Prohibition Law without calling the attention of the police to the existence of the place. In order not to have the cops come and nab you, you had to "speak easy."

Spendthrift. *What is the origin of the word "spend-thrift"?*

A "spendthrift" is one who "spends" the "thrift"—that is, the "savings"—of another. The term was first applied to the young man who upon inheriting his father's fortune immediately spent it.

Sphinx. *How did the Sphinx get its name?*

The name is Greek and means "the strangler." The "Sphinx" got her name because, according to legend, she strangled the travelers who could not solve the riddle she propounded. Though the name is Greek the legend is Egyptian; and though the Sphinx of the legend is a woman the famous Sphinx statue of Egypt bears the head of a man.

Spick. *Where did we get "spick" as a nickname for a foreigner?*

It's Navy slang and a variant of "spiggoty." This name for a foreigner—particularly a native of a Latin-American country—was given to the natives of Central America and South America because of their frequent use of the phrase, "No spick-a dee *Ingles.*"

Spite Curl. *What is the origin of the term "spite curl"?*

To enhance a woman's beauty a little curl was once plastered to the head by spit. This soon came to be jocularly referred to as a "spit curl." The "spit" was changed to "spite" in allusion to the poem written by Henry Wadsworth Longfellow in an attempt to teach Blanche Roosevelt how to pronounce "forehead":
"There was a little girl and she had a little curl
Right in the middle of her forehead;
When she was good, she was very, very good,
But when she was bad she was horrid."

Spittin' Image. *Why do we call a very close resemblance "the very spittin' image"?*

The expression is a corruption of the earlier phrase, "the very spit and image." It referred to two people so similar

228

that even their "spit" was alike. The change to "spittin'" came about from the general proclivity among boys, at least of an earlier generation, to try to "spit" like their fathers.

Splice the Main Brace. *Where did we get the expression "splice the main brace" as a synonym for taking a drink?* The term is nautical and there's a certain amount of humor attached to it. Any "brace" or rope that is worn can be strengthened by "splicing. " Similarly, a man is strengthened by strong drink—and so, to "splice the main brace" is to serve out grog.

Spruce Up. *What is the origin of the expression "spruce up"?* "Spruce" literally means "like the Prussians." It's from the French word for Prussia, *Prusse*. "Spruce fir" is the Prussian fir tree; "spruce beer" is beer made from the Prussian fir. And so, to "spruce up" is to "dress like a Prussian."

Stalking-Horse. *Where did we get the name "stalking-horse" for a person used as a cover or decoy?* From hunting. One method of stalking game in an open field is to walk along hidden by your horse; a horse used in this manner is a "stalking horse." From this we get the name—and our present meaning of a person used to cover the true aims of an organization or proceeding.

Stall Off. *Why do we say we "stall off" an impending event?* A "stall" is a decoy bird. From this, the person who assisted a pickpocket by diverting the attention of the victim came to be called a "stall." We use the term to mean "playing for time" because the pickpocket's assistant's two chief duties are to distract attention and play for time.

Stamping Ground. *How did a common gathering place come to be called a "stamping ground"?*
The allusion is to the fact that deer and other animals often have special spots which they visit day after day. Since you can detect such a spot by observing the ground —it's generally pretty much disturbed by the stamping hooves—it's called a "stamping ground."

Star Chamber. *Where did we get the expression "star chamber proceedings"?*
"Star chamber" as a name for a court of justice that is more arbitrary than just comes from an ancient English high court of that name noted for its arbitrary methods and rules. It was called the "Star Chamber" because "stars" were painted on the ceiling of the "chamber" in which the judges met.

Starboard. *What is the reason the "right" side of a ship is called "starboard"?*
The term comes from the Old English *steor-bord*, meaning "steering side"—because early sailing ships all had the steering oar placed on the right side.

Steal One's Thunder. *Who first accused someone else of "stealing his thunder"?*
The playwright Dennis, about the year 1700. Dennis said that he had invented a sound-effects machine which

230

could produce "thunder" off stage and complained that his rivals had "stolen his thunder." The idea of someone's stealing thunder so tickled the fancy of people that the phrase was adopted into the language.

Steeplechase. *Why is a horse race over obstacles called a "steeplechase"?*

Fox hunting gave us the term. If during a fox hunt no fox was found or the fox got away, some member of the hunt was likely to say, "I'll race you to the next town," and point to its most distinctive feature at a distance— the church steeple. The hunters would then start off, no longer on a fox chase, but on a "steeple chase." From this, any race over barriers is called a "steeplechase."

Steward. *How did a caretaker come to be called a "steward"?*

Originally the "steward" was employed to take care of pigs and cattle—because at one time these were the most important sources of wealth for the Saxon landlords. "Steward" comes from the Anglo-Saxon word *stig-weard* meaning "sty-keeper."

Stickler. *Why is a fuss-budget called a "stickler" for details?*

Because the Middle English word from which it's derived, *stightlen,* means "to set in order." Originally "sticklers" were judges at duels who saw to it that the rules of fair play were closely observed. Today, the "stickler" still follows rules very closely; he allows no deviation whatsoever.

231

Stogie. *How did the cigar called a "stogie" get that name?*

It was named for the Conestoga wagon—which was first built in the Conestoga valley in Lancaster County, Pennsylvania. Before the Revolution, the drivers of the Conestoga wagons took along with them on their long trips leaves of Lancaster County tobacco and rolled them into thin ropes for smoking. These were soon known as "Conestogas" and then as "stogies."

Stooge. *What is the origin of the word "stooge"?*

"Stooge" was originally a theatrical term and was first used to designate a comedian's accomplice hidden in the audience. From the fact that his real identity and purpose were not known to the other members of the audience he came to be called a "stool pigeon"—which, by elision, became "stooge."

Stool Pigeon. *Where did the "stool pigeon" get that name?*

The original "stool pigeons" were real pigeons seated on stools. They were used by pigeon hunters who, when they went out to net passenger pigeons for market, would tie a captive pigeon to a stool placed in front of the net. Then with strings attached to the stool pigeons' wings they'd make them flap—and so entice other pigeons into the net.

Strait-Laced. *What is the reason a priggish person is called "strait-laced"?*

Because a person wearing a "strait-laced" corset is "hemmed in" and cannot unbend. "Straight" is from the Latin *strictus*, meaning "tight" or "drawn close."

Stumped. *Why do we say a person who is unable to answer a question is "stumped"?*

When a person is "stumped" he's outwitted; and in the game of cricket the pitcher who has succeeded in hitting the wicket or "stump" has outwitted the batter.

Sucker. *How did a gullible person come to be called a "sucker"?*

A rather stupid fish is called a "sucker"—because it "sucks up" its food. It will just as complacently suck in live food, garbage, or a worm dangled in front of it on a hook. A person who, like the fish, complacently swallows the bait is also a "sucker."

Sundae. *Where and when did the ice cream "sundae" get that name?*

In the 1890's at E. C. Berners' ice-cream store in Two Rivers, Wisconsin. One night Berners sold a dish of vanilla ice cream to a boy named George Hallauer. George saw a bottle of chocolate syrup which was used for sodas and had a great idea. "Put some of that chocolate syrup over this ice cream," he said. Berners complied. Other customers tried it and liked it. Soon the combination became very popular in Two Rivers and spread to other towns, including Manitowoc—where George Giffy began offering it to the customers of his ice-cream store. The only drawback was the expense of selling both syrup and ice cream for a nickel. So Giffy and the others got together and decided to sell this dessert for a nickel on "Sundays" only. Shortly afterwards a little girl came into Giffy's store and said, "I want a nickel's worth of ice cream with stuff on it." Giffy explained that he sold it

233

for a nickel only on Sunday. "Then," said the girl, "this must be Sunday because I want that kind." The joke went around and soon the new dish was commonly called a "Sunday." The change in the spelling of the word came about at a later date and was the invention of an unknown merchant who wished to make the concoction seem more "fancy."

Supercilious. *Why do we call a haughty person "supercilious"?*
Because in Latin *super* means "above" and *cilium* means "eyebrow." A supercilious person goes about with "raised eyebrows."

Swab. *What is the origin of "swab" as a nickname for a seafaring man?*
Washing down the decks of their vessels was once one of the major peacetime occupations of navy men. To do this they used a mop or "swab." So the sailors were called "swabs." But the sailors did not apply this term to themselves; instead, observing the similarity in appearance between their mops and their officers' epaulets, they called their officers "swabs."

Swap. *Why do we call an exchange of goods a "swap"?*
"Swap" was originally a horse trader's term; it's a shortening of the phrase "swap a bargain." "Swap" means "strike."

Swashbuckler. *How did a romantic hero come to be called a "swashbuckler"?*
A "buckler" is a small shield and to "swash" is to "swish." A "swashbuckler" "swishes" his sword and rattles it on his shield or "buckler."

234

QUIZ 8

(Answers on page 280)

1. Why do we call an unpleasant person a "prune" or a "lemon"?
2. How did salted beef come to be called "corned beef"?
3. Why do we use the expression "on the Q.T." to mean "very quietly"?
4. What is the reason we say small boys "shinny" up a tree?
5. How did a single lock of hair in the middle of the head come to be called a "scalp lock"?
6. Why do we say a worthy person is "worth his salt"?
7. What is the origin of the expression "strike while the iron is hot"?
8. How did a confidence man come to be called a "slicker"?
9. Why do we call political speechmaking "stumping"?
10. What is the origin of the term "siesta"?
11. What is the reason a party for a bride-to-be is called a "shower"?
12. Why do we say a person caught in some nefarious act is caught "red-handed"?
13. How did a "wife" get that name?
14. What is the reason a careless person or his work is called "slipshod"?
15. Why do we call the odd or unusual "outlandish"?
16. What is the origin of the expression "spike his guns"?
17. How did we come to say that people with radically different opinions are "poles apart"?
18. Why do we say someone with knowledge or understanding has "savvy"?
19. What is the reason an effeminate person is called a "sissy"?
20. Why do we say the person who starts a project "does the groundwork"?

```
T T T T T T
T               T
T     T         T
T               T
T T T T T T
```

Table d'Hôte. *Why do we call a fixed-price meal a "table d'hôte"?*

The term is French and literally means "table of the host." During the Middle Ages almost all public eating-places were operated on what is now called the American plan. Guests sat at the "table of the host," took whatever was offered, and had to pay for the entire meal no matter what they ate. And so, "table d'hôte" came to signify "a complete meal at a fixed price."

Take the Cake. *Where did we get the expression "that takes the cake"?*

From the competitive cakewalk. This dance originated among the Negroes of the South—and got its name from the fact that at barbecues, picnics, and box suppers a strutting contest was held among the men. The man who cut the best capers in "strutting his stuff" was given his choice of cakes—and along with the cake went the girl who baked it as partner for the meal.

Take a Gander. *Why do we use the phrase "take a gander" to mean "take a look"?*

The month after a wife's confinement was once called the "gander month" or "gander moon"—in allusion to the

236

aimless wandering of a gander while the goose sits on the eggs. During this period the husband was called a "gander mooner"—and pleaded a certain amount of indulgence in matters pertaining to sex. So, originally, to "take a gander" was to "take a walk and give the girls the eye" as a "gander mooner" would do. The phrase as we use it today retains some of this meaning.

Take a Tip. *How did "take a tip" come to mean "take a hint"?*

This tip is from "tip off," which in turn comes from the expression "tip the wink"—that is, tilt the eyelid a bit to give a hint.

Talk Turkey. *Why do we say when a person gets down to the point that he's "talking turkey"?*

It's an allusion to an anecdote. An Indian and a white man went hunting and agreed that they would share the game equally. They bagged three crows and two wild turkeys. The white man divided their bag and gave his hunting companion the first bird—a crow. Then he took a turkey for himself, gave the Indian a crow, took the other turkey and gave the Indian the last bird—a crow. When the Indian objected, the white man pointed out that the Indian had three birds to his two. To which the Indian replied, "We stop talk birds; we now 'talk turkey.' "

Tantalize. *What is the origin of the word "tantalize"?*

"Tantalus" was the name of a son of Zeus; he was also a Lydian king. He made the mistake of revealing the secrets of the gods to the people on earth; he made the additional mistake of bringing down from Olympus the

237

food and drink of the gods—nectar and ambrosia—and offering them to mortals. As punishment he was condemned to stand in water up to his chin while right above his head hung a cluster of luscious grapes. When he got thirsty and tried to drink the water it receded; when he became hungry and tried to taste the grapes they moved just beyond his grasp. Thus he was "tantalized."

Tawdry. *How did something cheap and gaudy come to be called "tawdry"?*

At the annual fair held in honor of St. Audrey on the island of Ely a very cheap and gaudy lace was once sold; it was called "St. Audrey's lace." With time the first two words were run together and became "tawdry."

Taxi. *What is the reason a "taxi" is called that?*

The word originally referred to the "meter" carried by the cab. It was called a "taximeter" because it measured the fare or "tax"—and cabs equipped with them proudly boasted of the fact by painting "taximeter" on their doors. This was soon shortened to "taxi" and in time all cabs were called that.

Teetotaler. *Where did we get the name "teetotaler" for a total abstainer?*

The word seems to have originated with the doubling of the "T" for emphasis but it came into widespread use through its association with a temperance campaign. Members of a temperance society—perhaps the one organized at Hector, New York, in 1815—pledged themselves to abstain from distilled spirits. Later, another

238

pledge was circulated which bound the signers to total abstinence. The two classes of signers were distinguished by the initials "O.P.," standing for "Old Pledge," and "T," for "Total Abstainer." The movement took hold and spread throughout America and the British Isles—with men signing a "T–Total" pledge.

Tell It to the Marines. *How did we get the saying "tell it to the Marines"?*
This expression grew out of the sailors' feeling of superiority to the marines. Marines, in their opinion, are so green they will swallow any extravagant tale; and so, the phrase means: "Tell that to greenhorns and not to men who know better."

Terrier. *Why is a "terrier" called that?*
Because the Latin word for "earth" is *terra*. Therefore the home of a fox or badger—being a hole in the earth—is a "terrier." And because of this, a dog trained to chase a fox or badger from its "terrier" is called a "terrier."

Thimble. *How did the "thimble" get that name?*
The "thimble" was at first worn on the thumb; and, since it's shaped like a bell, it was called a "thumb-bell."

Third Degree. *What is the origin of the term "third degree"?*
The term alludes to Freemasonry. In order to become a "Third Degree" Mason, a candidate must pass a simple test. But many years ago uninformed persons who were not Masons got the idea that this test was very difficult; they believed it to be a nerve-racking mental and physical ordeal. Though this was untrue the popular concep-

tion persisted and the term "third degree" ultimately became synonymous with the severe police questioning of a reluctant prisoner.

Three Sheets in the Wind. *Where does the phrase "three sheets in the wind" come from?*

From sailing. The sails of a ship are fastened at one "bottom corner" by a "tack" which is more or less fixed and at the other by a "sheet" which can be unloosened. Most commercial sailing vessels have three sails, each with its separate sheet, and when one of these "sheets" becomes loose the sail flaps back and forth and is said to be "in the wind." If all three sheets are "in the wind," the ship and sails move about without purpose—as the wind blows them. So, a person reeling drunkenly about is said to have "three sheets in the wind."

Throw in the Sponge. *How did the expression "throw in the sponge" come to be used as an acknowledgment of defeat?*

In the early days of boxing a contestant's seconds would toss into the center of the ring the "sponge" with which they had wiped his face—as a sign that their man could not continue and they admitted defeat. The practice is continued today—except that a towel is substituted for the "sponge."

Thug. *Why are criminals sometimes called "thugs"?*

The original "thugs" were members of a professional gang of thieves and murderers in India who made a practice of strangling their victims. The word is from the Hindustani *thag*, meaning a "cheat" or "swindler."

Tickled to Death. *What is the origin of the expression "tickled to death"?*

Legend has it that there was an old form of Chinese punishment and torture in which the victim was literally just "tickled to death." If this was true, then it is presumably possible to so tickle the fancy of a person that he too will die.

Tin Lizzie. *How did the "tin lizzie" get that name?*

Ford automobiles were called "Lizzie" by personification—the name probably having been chosen because of its similarity to "lizard." If a person with a fast car has a "whizzer," then a person with a slow car, has a "lizard"—or "lizzie." "Tin" is used to indicate the cheapness of the car—the sheet steel used in making tin cans being the thinnest commonly known.

Tinker's Dam. *Why do we say something that is worth little is "not worth a tinker's dam"?*

Because a "tinker's dam" is just about as worthless as anything can be. When a tinker is preparing a vessel for soldering he will make a little "dam" out of clay or earth to keep the solder from spreading; when the solder has hardened he throws the dam away. It is this "dam" the phrase refers to.

Tip. *What is the reason we call a gratuity a "tip"?*

Years ago in English inns and taverns it was customary for the patrons to drop a coin for the benefit of the waiters into a box placed on the wall. On the box was a little sign which said: "To insure promptness." Later just the initials of the phrase were put on the box—T.I.P.

241

Tittle. *Why do we use the word "tittle" in the expression "not a jot or tittle"?*

Just as the "jot" or "iota" was a dot below a vowel, the "tittle" is the dot above the "i" or "j." These dots are just about the smallest things that can be written—and so "not a jot or tittle" means "not even the very least."

Toady. *What is the original of the term "toady"?*

The original "toady" was the magician's assistant who ate toads so that his master could demonstrate his magical healing powers—since at one time toads were considered poisonous. The other duties of the "toad-eater" were very much like those of the "yes man" of today —to prove the boss right—and so we got the word and its meaning.

Toast. *How did the word "toast" get into the expression "drink a toast"?*

The "toast" was once in the glass. The custom was to place a small piece of toast in the bottom of the glass as a delicacy. And since in drinking to a person you drained your glass, you "drank" this bit of "toast."

Tommy Atkins. *Where did the British soldier get the nickname "Tommy Atkins"?*

"Thomas Atkins" was the specimen name used by the British Army in its official regulations of 1815. One sheet, for instance, was headed "Description of Service of Thomas Atkins"; another, "Clothing Account of Thomas Atkins"; and a bounty receipt was made out, "Received, Thomas Atkins, His 'X' Mark."

Tommyrot. *Why do we call something that's worthless "tommyrot"?*

The term comes from the use of "tommy" to mean "food." Since loaves of bread were once distributed in England by charity on "St. Thomas' Day," the twenty-first of December, this bread was called "tommy." Then, British soldiers began calling all their food "tommy" because it was issued to them much as the bread was distributed. Perhaps this food wasn't very good to begin with; in any event it was worthless when rotten.

Tout. *What is the reason a race-track tipster is called a "tout"?*

The word "tout" is a dialect form of "toot"—from the Anglo-Saxon *totian,* meaning "to stick out." The first "touts" were men who stuck their heads out of their shops in search of business. Later, bookmakers employed touts to give people tips on the races—and then tell them where they could place their bets.

Trade Winds. *How did the "trade winds" get that name?*

This particular "trade" comes from the Old German *trata* which literally means "track." The "trade winds" follow a uniform "track."

Tram. *Where did the British get the name "tram" for a steetcar?*

From the German *traam,* meaning "the handle of a dung-sledge or wheelbarrow." The term was adopted by English miners to designate the vehicle they used for carrying ore. And the first railways were not built in the streets but in the mines—where they were used to carry the miners' "trams."

243

Tried in the Balance. *What is the origin of the expression "tried in the balance and found wanting"?*
The expression refers to the ancient Egyptian belief that the soul of the deceased was weighed and its weight determined the fate he would suffer.

Trousseau. *Why do we call the clothes a bride takes with her on her honeymoon her "trousseau"?*
The term comes from the French *trusse*, which means "little bundle." In early times the "trousseau" was a little bundle of household things which the wife took with her to her new home; it was in the nature of a dowry.

True Blue. *What is the origin of the expression "true blue"?*
The term originally referred to the blue aprons and jackets once worn by butchers, which did not show blood stains. But it got its present meaning from the adoption of blue as the color of the pro-Parliament Scottish Presbyterian Party of the seventeenth century—in contradistinction to the royal red.

Trump Card. *How did a special card or suit of cards come to be called "trump"?*
The word "trump" is a corruption of "triumph." A "trump" is a card which can "triumph" or win over other cards in the game by virtue of its special powers.

Tumbler. *What is the reason we call certain drinking glasses "tumblers"?*
It's because at one time these drinking glasses really "tumbled." They were made with a pointed or curved base so that you could not set them down until you had drained them to the last drop.

Tura-Lura. *Why do so many songs have phrases like "tura-lura" and "tirralirra" in them?*

These terms come from *turelure*, the French word for the music of the bagpipes. They were first inserted in songs as a vocalise filling in for an accompanying instrument.

Turkey. *How did our native American bird get the name "turkey"?*

Guinea hens and cocks were first imported into England from Africa by way of the Turkish dominions—and so were called "Turkey" cocks and hens. When the American bird was introduced it was confused with the African and given the same name. Then, when a distinction between the two birds was finally established and the names were differentiated, "turkey" was erroneously retained for the American bird instead of the African.

Turn Down. *What is the reason we say something rejected is "turned down"?*

The phrase is derived from the old custom of turning down an empty glass when no more drink is desired—but a more direct antecedent was the "courting mirror" used in colonial days. This was a small hand mirror used by bashful swains to help them propose. The young man would bring a "courting mirror" to the home of his sweetheart and place it face upward on the table. This action informed the young lady that he wished to marry her. If her answer to this proposal of marriage was "yes" she would smile at his image in the mirror. But if it were "no" she would "turn" the mirror, and therefore his image, face "down."

245

Turn a Hair. *Where did we get the expression "he didn't turn a hair"?*

It comes from horse racing. A horse that had won a race without having its coat roughed up by sweat was said to have won without "turning a hair."

Turncoat. *Why is a traitor called a "turncoat"?*

In allusion to a literal turning of the coat inside out that was the custom in the days when feudal lords maintained their own armies. Each lord had a special livery for his servants and swordsmen and when a man left one lord for the service of another, he turned his livery coat inside out so that he might not be mistaken for an enemy upon approaching the castle of his new master.

Turnip. *How did pocket watches come to be called "turnips"?*

"Turnip" as a name for a watch—which was rather appropriate when all watches were almost that big—was suggested by that old Mother Goose rhyme:

> "If wishes were horses,
> Beggars would ride;
> If turnips were watches,
> I'd wear one by my side."

Turnpike. *Where did main highways get the name "turnpikes"?*

The name comes from the poles or bars—that is "pikes"—which were once swung on a pivot across the roads and had to be "turned" before vehicles or horsemen could pass. They were set up to insure the collection of tolls on the highways.

Tuxedo. *Why do we use the word "tuxedo" when referring to a man's evening jacket?*

Because it was first worn at Tuxedo Park in Orange County, New York. But, according to legend, this coat was devised by King Edward VII of England while he was still Prince of Wales. As a young man, Edward liked to play cards and would often sit all night at the table—where, being rather stout, his full-dress coattails got in his way. So Edward had a coat made up with the tails clipped off, and that's how the tuxedo came into being.

Twenty-Three, Skiddoo. *What is the origin of the expression "twenty-three, skiddoo"?*

In 1899 Henry Miller presented in New York a dramatization of Dickens' "Tale of Two Cities" called "The Only Way." In the last act of this play, an old woman sat at the foot of the guillotine, counting the heads as they were lopped off. The only attention she paid to the execution of Sidney Carton was to remark—as his head fell from the guillotine—"Twenty-three." This bit of dramatic irony caught on with theatrical people, became telegraphers' slang for "bad news," and was ultimately combined with "skiddoo" by T. A. Dorgan, the cartoonist. "Skiddoo" is just a fanciful variant of "skedaddle."

Two Bits. *Why do we call a quarter "two bits"?*

Our dollar was originally based on the Spanish dollar and the Spanish dollar was divided into eight parts—whence "pieces of eight." In the West Indies, where Spanish money was widely used, Spanish paper dollars were often cut up into eight parts—and each of these bits of paper was called a "bit." One of these "bits" was equal to twelve and a half cents in American money. So, a 25-cent piece was the equivalent of "two bits."

Two Strings to His Bow. *Where does the expression "two strings to his bow" come from?*

From England. British archers long followed the prudent practice of carrying a spare bowstring when they went to war. A man who had "two strings to his bow" was certainly doubly prepared.

Tycoon. *How did a person of importance come to be called a "tycoon"?*

The name comes from the Japanese *tai*, meaning "great," and *kun*, meaning "prince." The Japanese have never used the word among themselves, however; they use it only when speaking to foreigners in an attempt to impress them with their own importance and the sovereignty of their ruler. Commodore Perry brought the word back from Japan with him in 1854.

U U U U U U U
U U
U U U
U U
U U U U U U U

U-Boat. *Why do we call the German submarine a "U-boat"?*

Because the German name for a "submarine" is *unterseeboot*—and so, the "U" stands for "undersea."

Umbrage. *What is the reason we say a person who takes offense takes "umbrage"?*

The word "umbrage" comes from the Latin *umbra*, meaning "shadow." A shadow is a "dark picture"—"a gloomy view," as it were—and a person who takes umbrage "believes the worst."

Umpire. *Where does the word "umpire" come from?*

From the Old French word *nompair*, meaning "not paired." The "umpire" is the third or "not paired" person called upon to decide between two contestants.

Uncle. *Why do we call a pawnbroker "uncle"?*

As a humorous pun on the Latin word *uncus*, meaning "hook." At one time pledges of clothing were hung on a hook or *uncus* in the pawnbroker's shop; his shop was therefore called *uncus*—and it's but a short step from that to "uncle's."

Uncle Sam. *How did "Uncle Sam" get his name?*

The original "Uncle Sam"—goatee, twinkling eye, and all—was Samuel Wilson, born in West Cambridge, Massachusetts. In time, he moved with his brother Ebenezer to Troy, New York, where they formed a partnership in the meat-packing business. The brothers contracted to supply the Army with beef and pork during the War of 1812, and marked their shipping barrels "U.S." The soldiers jokingly called the meat "Uncle Sam's" beef or pork—since "Uncle Sam" Wilson's first two initials coincided with the "U.S." marking on the barrels. A soldier drew a caricature of Sam Wilson with his goatee and flowing hair and labeled the picture, "Uncle Sam of the U.S.A." This picture was the original of the ones used to depict "Uncle Sam" today. The first "Uncle Sam" died in Troy on July 31, 1854, and lies beside his brother, Ebenezer, in the Miller plot at Oakwood Cemetery. A monument has been erected in Troy to his memory.

Under the Weather. *What is the reason we say a person who is feeling ill is feeling "under the weather"?*

It's because the greenhorn aboard a ship who feels slightly seasick seeks shelter from the wind by crouching down beside the bulwarks—"under" their protection—on the "weather" or windy side of the ship.

Up Salt River. *How did the expression "up Salt River" come to mean "out of luck"?*

This phrase is no doubt a euphemism—but it has persisted because of the story told in connection with it. In the 1832 Presidential contest between Henry Clay and Andrew Jackson, Clay employed a boatman to row him up the Ohio River to Louisville where he was scheduled to make a speech. The boatman, being a Jackson man, "accidentally on purpose" lost his way and rowed Clay up the branch of the Ohio known as the "Salt River," thus keeping him from his engagement. By the time the 1840 campaign rolled around, one of the popular campaign songs used "Up Salt River" as a refrain—still, most probably, with the euphemism in mind.

Up to Scratch. *What is the reason we say a person who comes up to our expectations comes "up to scratch"?*
The expression comes from prize fighting. At one time a line was scratched on the ground with the toe and the fighters had to come up to it to fight. But neither could go beyond it—so one who wished to default just failed to "come up to the scratch." The practice of scratching a line on the ground is followed by young boys to this day.

Up to Snuff. *Why do we use the phrase "up to snuff" to mean "up to par"?*
The expression was first used to describe a person's physical condition. The most sensitive of all our senses is that of smell. It's the one most easily upset by our general physical condition. So a person who said he was "up to snuff" meant he was able to "sniff," or "smell"— in other words, in fine condition.

Upbraid. *How did "upbraid" come to mean "rebuke"?*
"Upbraid" comes from the Anglo-Saxon word, *up-bregdan*, which means "to draw up." When you "upbraid" a person you "draw him up" to the line of proper behavior and make him "toe the mark."

251

Upper Crust. *Why do we call high society the "upper crust"?*

Because the "crust" was long considered the best part of the bread and the "upper" or top crust the best part of all. If "high society" is the best of all, then it's "upper crust."

Upstage. *What is the reason we use the word "upstage" to mean "snobbish"?*

Because in the theatre "upstage" refers to the rear of the stage and at one time the rear was higher than the front. Since the actor standing "upstage" stood higher than the rest, this was the traditional position for the actor-king—and any other actor going upstage was pretending to an exalted position he did not deserve.

Utopia. *How did the ideal come to be called "utopia"?*

The term is from the Greek *où* and *tópos* which, literally translated, means "not a place"—that is, "nowhere." The word was devised by Sir Thomas More who wrote a book entitled: "A fruteful and Pleasaunt Worke of the best State of a Publyque Weale, and of the newe Yle called Utopia."

Vamp. *Why are seductive women and firemen both called "vamps"?*

A seductive woman is called a "vamp" in allusion to the "vampire" of folk lore—a ghostly being that supposedly sucked the blood of living persons. A fireman is called a "vamp" because at one time in England "vamp" meant "to tramp" or "walk"—and the volunteer firemen generally went to the fires on foot.

Vandal. *What is the reason a person who needlessly destroys property is called a "vandal"?*

The term gets its meaning from a Teutonic tribe. In 455 A.D. Genseric and his "Vandal" hordes captured Rome and mutilated the public monuments of the city without regard to their worth or beauty.

Vaudeville. *How did "vaudeville" get its name?*

The word is French and comes from the phrase *"chanson du Vau de Vire,"* meaning "a song of the Valley of Vire." The Vire is a river in Normandy and in the fifteenth century Olivier Basselin, a fuller of that region, composed a number of light satirical songs that became very popular.

253

Ventriloquism. *Where did we get the term "ventriloquism" as a name for "throwing the voice"?*

The word comes from the Latin and literally means "to speak from the belly"—*venter* meaning "the belly," and *loqui* meaning "to speak." The Romans thought that ventriloquists spoke by using the air in their stomachs.

Vestal Virgin. *Why do we call an extremely chaste woman a "vestal virgin"?*

Because the maidens who served the Roman goddess, "Vesta" were required to be absolutely chaste and were therefore called "vestal virgins."

Vicar. *What is the reason we use "vicar" as a synonym for "minister"?*

The term comes from the Latin *vicarius*, meaning "substitute." The original idea behind its use was that the vicar "substituted" for Christ in interpreting the words of God.

Villain. *How did a "villain" come to be called that?*

In feudal times this term meant "one attached to the villa"—that is, "the manor house." The notion of wickedness grew out of the assumption on the part of the feudal lord of the manor that all servants were knaves.

Volume. *Why is a book called a "volume"?*

Ancient books were written on sheets of paper which were fastened together lengthwise and rolled up like a window shade. "Volume" is from the Latin *volvere*, meaning "to roll up."

254

QUIZ 9

(Answers on page 282)

1. *Why do we say two things that fit together exactly "fit to a T"?*
2. *How did a sailor come to be called a "tar"?*
3. *What is the origin of the expression "put one's shoulder to the wheel"?*
4. *Why do we call an exaggeration a "fish story"?*
5. *How did the "guinea hen" get that name?*
6. *What is the reason an approaching storm is said to be "brewing"?*
7. *Why do we say a protective person takes another "under his wing"?*
8. *What is the origin of the expression "kick over the traces"?*
9. *Why is a person out-of-favor said to be "under a cloud"?*
10. *Where did we get "togs" as a name for clothes?*
11. *What is the origin of the expression "resting on one's oars"?*
12. *Why do we use the expression "yum-yum" to mean pleasant-tasting?*
13. *Where does the term "umbrella" come from?*
14. *Why do we say an actor "treads the boards"?*
15. *What is the reason we say a person has "an ax to grind" when we mean he has some hidden purpose in mind?*
16. *What is the origin of the expression "give a man enough rope"?*
17. *Why do we say a person who has been "taken down a peg" has "had his wings clipped"?*
18. *How did we get the expression "put up or shut up"?*
19. *What is the reason an outstanding success is called a "wow"?*
20. *Why do we call a celebrity a "bigwig"?*

```
W W W W W
W         W
W   W     W
W         W
W W W W W
```

Wac. *How did the "Wacs" come to be called that?*

From the initials of their full name—"Women's Army Corps." Originally, when their official title was "Women's Auxiliary Army Corps," they were known as "Waacs."

Wampum. *Where did "wampum" get its name?*

"Wampum" is an Algonquian Indian word, meaning "white string." There were two types of Indian bead money—white and black (or purple). The "white" was the more valuable.

Wash One's Hands. *Why do we speak of "washing our hands" of an affair we don't wish to be connected with?*

Because that's what Pontius Pilate did when he yielded to the people and condemned Jesus—although he found Him "not guilty." But the custom is far older; baptism is a "washing away of sins" and so are many more primitive customs.

Wash Out. *How did "wash out" come to mean a failure?*

In the early nineteenth century British soldiers learned marksmanship by shooting at iron targets. The marks, if they were not good enough, were painted out or "whitewashed." Thus a "wash out" came to mean a failure or a disappointment.

Water Wagon. *What is the origin of the expression "on the water wagon"?*

The term comes from the army where wagons carrying water once accompanied the troops on the march. After a heavy night of drinking and carousal a man was often in need of copious drinks of water—as well as inclined to swear off liquor for good. For this reason the man, literally as well as figuratively, "climbed on the water wagon."

Waves. *How did the "Waves" get this name?*

The name was selected arbitrarily by the Navy Department and then a phrase was found that would embody the letters W-A-V-E-S as initials—"Women Accepted for Volunteer Emergency Service."

Weasel Words. *Why do we call the words a person uses in an attempt to change his position "weasel words"?*

A "weasel" caught in a trap will try to squirm and wiggle its way out. "Weasel words" are words used in an attempt to get out of a tight situation.

Weather Eye. *How did we come to use the expression "keep your weather eye open" to mean "look out for danger"?*

The "weather eye" is the one which looks toward the wind—from which direction, as all sailors know, a change in weather will be indicated.

Welcher. *Why do we call a person who backs out of his commitments a "welcher"?*

The term was originally spelled "Welsher" and alludes to the old nursery rhyme: "Taffy was a Welshman, Taffy was a thief."

Welsh Rabbit. *What is the reason we call a dish made ot cheese "Welsh rabbit"?*

The term is humorous. The Welsh were supposed to be so poverty-stricken they could not afford even rabbit meat but had to substitute cheese for it.

Wet Blanket. *Why do we call a person who doesn't enter into the spirit of a party a "wet blanket"?*

A "wet blanket' will smother a fire—and a person who can't have fun at a party will have a similar effect.

Where's Elmer? *Where did the members of the American Legion get "Where's Elmer?" as their "battle cry"?*

At a California State Convention of the American Legion held in Oakland in 1932. The treasurer's name was Elmer and Legionnaires who wanted to get their checks cashed found they needed his signature. So, throughout the convention the cry was continually raised: "Where's Elmer?" This "battle cry" was carried by the California delegation to the national convention at Portland, Oregon, and was there adopted by the entire American Legion.

Whipping Boy. *What is the origin of the term "whipping boy"?*

When a king's son was bad he should, like any other boy, have been whipped. But because he was of royal blood

258

he couldn't be—and so it was once the custom to keep about the court some other "boy" who could be "whipped" instead of the prince.

White Elephant. *How did an onerous burden that cannot be dropped come to be called a "white elephant"?*
The allusion is to the story of an Eastern potentate who, when he wished to impoverish or destroy a courtier, presented him with one of the court's sacred "white elephants." The courtier then had to care for the elephant but could not put it to work—since it was sacred. The ultimate effect was to reduce the courtier to poverty.

White Feather. *Why do we speak of a cowardly deed as "showing the white feather"?*
When gamecocks are crossbred, a different colored "feather" shows up in their tails. This, more often than not, is "white." It is generally believed that any outside strain will lead to cowardice in a gamecock—and so an act of cowardice is called "showing the white feather."

Whole Cloth. *Why do we say an out-and-out lie is "made out of whole cloth"?*
You "spin" a yarn and "weave" the plot and from the "cloth" you make up a story. If it's made out of "whole cloth" it's all of a piece, all alike—usually, as we use the phrase today—without a bit of the "fabric" of truth.

Wide Berth. *What is the reason we say we give a "wide berth" to something we avoid?*
It's because the spot where a ship lies at anchor is called its "berth" and if it's been anchored so it can swing

259

freely with the wind and the tide and with all other ships at a distance, it has been given, quite literally, a "wide berth."

Wild-Goose Chase. *How did a "wild-goose chase" get that name?*

A "wild-goose chase" was once a sort of game—a horse race in which the second and each succeeding horse had to follow the leader accurately and at a definite interval. Since the horses had to keep their positions like geese in flight, the chase was called a "wild-goose chase"; and since this was no race—for no one could win—we adopted the phrase to describe a person following a course that leads to no goal.

Willies. *What is the origin of the expression "I've got the willies"?*

The term comes from "wiffle-woffles." "Wiffle-woffles" are "collie-woffles" or "collie-wobbles." If your stomach is upset, you have the "colic" and it seems to "wobble."

Win Hands Down. *Where did we get the expression "win hands down"?*

From horse racing. A jockey who doesn't have to raise his hands to tighten the reins or wield the whip to win— "wins hands down."

Wind Up. *Why do we say a frightened or alarmed person "gets the wind up"?*

The allusion is to a deer or other animal which will, if startled, raise its head to "get the wind up" its nostrils in an attempt to determine if any enemy is approaching.

260

Windfall. *How did a bit of unexpected good fortune come to be called a "windfall"?*

Certain members of the English nobility were forbidden by the tenure of their estates to fell any timber, all the trees being reserved for the use of the Royal Navy. They could, however, use any that were blown down by the wind—and so a "windfall" was unexpected good luck.

Wink Is as Good as a Nod. *Why do we say "a wink is as good as a nod"?*

The original phrase was, "A wink is as good as a nod to a blind horse." In other words, there's no point in nodding at a person who can't see you wink. But we have changed the meaning of this expression to indicate the ability to take a hint—and so, of necessity, have dropped all reference to the horse.

Wirepulling. *What is the reason we say a person who is using his friends and acquaintances to gain his ends is "wirepulling"?*

The first "wirepullers" were puppet masters. Then the term was applied to politicians who, like puppet masters, controlled the actions of those in office from behind the scenes. Today we apply the phrase "wirepulling" to those attempting to get others to "pull wires" for them.

Wisdom Teeth. *Why are our "wisdom teeth" called that?*

Because people were once supposed to have reached the "age of wisdom" when they cut these teeth. But certain persons never have any.

X-Y-Z X-Y-Z X-Y-Z X-Y-Z
X   X
Y X-Y-Z   Y
Z   Z
X-Y-Z X-Y-Z X-Y-Z X-Y-Z

Xmas. *Why is Christmas so often written "Xmas"?*

The "X" in this case is the Greek letter *chi*—written X —and *chi* is the initial letter of the Greek word for "Christ."

X-Ray. *How did the "X-ray" get that name?*

The ray was first called the "Roentgen ray" in honor of the scientist who discovered it. But he preferred to call it "X-ray" because "X" is the algebraic symbol for the unknown and at that time he did not understand the nature of this ray.

Yankee. *What is the origin of the term "Yankee"?*

The word comes from a nickname for the Dutch, *Jan Kaas*, meaning "John Cheese." Holland has long been famous for its cheeses and so the nickname *Jan Kaas*, or "John Cheese," is appropriate to them. In pirate days, English sailors adopted the term as a derisive name for the Dutch freebooters. In this sense it became familiar in New York. Then the Dutch settlers there—noting its unpleasant significance—began to apply it to the English settlers of Connecticut because they believed the Connecticut English to be far more enterprising than ethical. The term spread to the other colonies—though at first it was almost always used to refer with dislike to the citizens of a colony farther North. It still is in certain sections—often with a "damn" placed before it.

Yankee Dime. *Why do we call a kiss a "yankee dime"?*
This name for a kiss has its origin in our habit of attributing to other sections of the country such behavior and characteristics as we do not especially approve of. "Yankees" were said to be so thrifty that they would rather pay for something with a kiss than with a "coin." A kiss is also called a "Quaker fip" (that is, a five cent piece) for the same reason.

Yellow Press. *How did the term "yellow press" come to be applied to newspapers specializing in sensationalism?*
It's because in the late 1800's these papers began printing sensational articles about the "Yellow Peril"—the ever-increasing Chinese and Japanese population—which they said threatened the safety of the white race.

Zany. *Where did a fool get the name "zany"?*
In the plays performed by the Italian *commedia dell' arte*—in which the servants acted as clowns and bore the name *zani*. The word "zany" was first used in English to designate a comic performer attending on a clown—a "stooge."

Zest. *Why does "zest" mean "enthusiasm"?*
Because in its Greek form "zest" meant a piece of orange or lemon peel. And the addition of a slice of orange or lemon peel adds "zest" to a drink or dish—and makes us more enthusiastic about it.

263

QUIZ 10

(Answers on page 284)

1. Why do we call a dishwasher a "pearl diver"?
2. How did the "undertaker" get that name?
3. What is the reason we call out, "Gangway!" when we wish people to get out of our way?
4. Why do we call a man's formal dress his "soup and fish"?
5. What is the origin of the term "earmark"?
6. How did cigarettes get the name "coffin nails"?
7. Why do we say those who are unhappy "lead a dog's life"?
8. What is the reason a frying pan is called a "spider"?
9. How did the face come to be called the "phiz"?
10. Why do we say a group of persons walking in line are walking "Indian file"?
11. How did the girl's garment come to be called a "middy blouse"?
12. What is the reason we call an expert person a "past master"?
13. Why do we say that "one swallow does not make a summer"?
14. How did we get the expression "show his true colors"?
15. Where did we get the word "cent" for the hundredth part of a dollar?
16. Why do we say a person who has made a passably good showing "gave us a run for our money"?
17. What is the reason we call a gathering for work a "bee"?
18. How did a dandy come to be called a "buck"?
19. Why do we call the first team of a university the "varsity"?
20. How did "zwieback" get that name?

264

? ? ? ? ? ? ? ? ?
?   ?
? Answers ?
? To Quizzes ?
?   ?
? ? ? ? ? ? ? ? ? ?

A Note On Scoring: Do not attempt to score your answers on a percentage basis. The questions asked are too varied and cover too wide a field of acquired knowledge for a percentage score to be accurate.

Instead, count as correct any answer which embodies the general idea of the explanation given here—even though it does not include all the facts—and compare the total number of correct answers for each quiz with the following table:

15 or more correct	excellent
13 or 14 correct	very good
11 or 12 correct	good
9 or 10 correct	fair
8 or less correct	poor

ANSWERS—QUIZ 1

1. **All at Sea:** A person who doesn't know where he is going or what he is doing is like a ship which is out of sight of land and unable to determine its position. It, too, is "all at sea."
2. **Underhand:** The allusion is to cardsharps and magicians who, to practice their tricks, place their hands "under" the table.
3. **Atta Boy:** This is more than a phrase to cheer on a contestant. It is a shortening of the phrase "that's the boy"—meaning, "here's the man for the situation."
4. **Albumen:** The white of an egg is called "albumen" because the Latin word for "white" is *albus*.
5. **Soda Jerker:** The counterman behind the soda fountain "jerks" the handle of the dispenser towards him to produce the soda—and so is called a "soda jerker."
6. **Go like Blazes:** A good roaring fire can travel fast; but the "blazes" referred to here are the "blazes of Hell"—which undoubtedly go even faster.
7. **Bats in the Belfry:** The belfry at the top of the church corresponds to the head atop the human body. Bats will take up their abode in a belfry that is empty and cavernous—likewise, by analogy, in an empty head.
8. **Bristle:** When alarmed, a hedgehog will raise the bristles on its back; a dog, the hackles of its neck; and a human, sometimes, the hair of his head.
9. **Beachcomber:** A loafer on the shores of an island in the South Seas or an idle tramp who lives on what he can pick up on the beach "combs" it for treasure trove, and so is a "beachcomber."

10. **Sprig:** A young man or boy is not yet a branch on the family tree—he's just a "sprig."

11. **Broadcloth:** The reference was originally to its width, not its quality. It required two weavers, sitting side by side, to fling the shuttle all the way across the cloth.

12. **Raise the Roof:** The expression comes from the theatre. If the applause and cheers of the audience are loud enough, they not only "bring down the house," but also "raise the roof."

13. **Take the Bit in His Teeth:** The "bit" of a horse's bridle pinches his cheek; this hurts—and so he turns. But if the horse "takes the bit in his teeth" he can prevent its hurting —and so need pay no attention to his driver's tugging on the reins.

14. **Bully:** The person who boasts and is overbearing is called a "bully" because he bellows like a bull—and is just as "mean." (When this word means "jolly" or "nice," it comes from the German *buhle*, meaning "a lover.")

15. **Bury the Hatchet:** Among certain tribes of American Indians it was the custom to declare peace after a war by taking a war hatchet or tomahawk and ceremonially burying it.

16. **Brand Spanking New:** Just as the "brand" of this expression refers to the fire in which a smith heats the metal he is working on, so the "spanking" refers to his hammering the metal.

17. **Bus:** This term is a shortening of "omnibus"—which in Latin means "for all." A bus is a common carrier "for all."

18. **Ragging:** Since the tongue is humorously called "the red rag," a scold "waves the red rag." And since the scold is nagging, the scolding is "ragging." British schoolboys first applied this term to verbal hazing.

19. **On the Ball:** In almost all games played with a ball, it is essential for the player—in order not to be caught flat-

267

footed away from where he should be—to "keep his eye on the ball." Thus, any alert person is said to be "on the ball."

20. **In the Bag:** When you are hunting, the game you see may escape—but the game you've already shot and put "in the bag" is sure.

❧

ANSWERS—QUIZ 2

1. **Cat Nap:** A cat while playing with a mouse that it's caught will pretend to sleep, hoping the mouse will start to get away and so give the cat even more fun in playing with it.

2. **Chip In:** The term comes from the game of poker. There is a central pot or ante in the game to which each player is supposed to add chips, or "chip in."

3. **Chiseler:** A chisel is used to pry boards apart, and a "chiseler" pries a man and his customer apart—by quoting lower prices or other "unethical" means.

4. **Christmas:** The word is just a shortened form of "Christ's mass."

5. **Left-Handed Compliment:** The general supposition is that anything done with the left hand is done poorly and awkwardly—and so a "left-handed compliment" is one that's really no compliment at all.

6. **Cootie:** The term was originally "cutie." During World War I a soldier searching his clothing for lice would hold up a big, fat specimen and exclaim, "Ain't he a cutie?"

7. **He's a Corker:** You can keep a bottle of beer from foaming by placing a cork in it. If you can stop a person who's ranting and "foaming at the mouth" by some state-

268

ment that leaves him speechless—you, by analogy, are a "corker."

8. **Cocksure:** The term alludes to a gamecock. There's no animal or bird that seems more sure of himself than the strutting "cock of the walk"—he's "cocky" and "cocksure."

9. **Cotton Up:** Cotton lint sticks very closely to our clothes —and a girl who likes a boy will stick just as closely to him.

10. **Cowlick:** The term comes from a common milk barn experience. When a cow, out of undue affection, licks your head, it leaves your hair standing on end like a "cowlick."

11. **Knocked into a Cocked Hat:** A cocked hat is an ordinary round hat that has been intentionally pressed out of its original shape. To be "knocked into a cocked hat" is to be forced out of shape—unintentionally.

12. **Hot Dog:** The term comes from the popular notion that anything might be thrown into the machine—even dogs— and then sold as frankfurters.

13. **Do-Re-Mi:** If just an ordinary amount of money is "dough," then a more than ordinary amount can be indicated by going up the scale—"do-re-mi."

14. **Bring to Heel:** Properly trained dogs are taught to follow at their master's heel on command. When they start scampering about too much he will bring them "to heel" by such a command and make them "dog his footsteps."

15. **I'll Be a Dutchman if I Do:** To be a Dutchman is, of course, the worst possible fate—under the general idea of the Dutch embodying all evil. So, to say "I'll be a Dutchman if I do" is to indicate that not even this fate will alter the decision.

16. **Sing:** If a prisoner is a "jailbird" or a "canary"—then when he opens his mouth he most logically "sings."

269

17. **Crust:** The crust is the tough, thick "skin" of a loaf of bread. If a person is brash, he too has a thick skin—he has "crust."

18. **I'll Lead You a Pretty Dance:** The phrase has its origin in early English dances—many of which were a form of "follow the leader"—and so the reference is obvious.

19. **Dead as a Smoked Herring:** There could hardly be a fish more surely dead—since a smoked herring is gutted, beheaded, and then smoked for hours.

20. **Drunk as a Lord:** The general belief among the peasants of England was that the vices of the nobility were far greater than their own. So, to be "as drunk as a lord" was to have reached the ultimate in drunkenness.

ANSWERS—QUIZ 3

1. **Feather One's Nest:** The person who "feathers his nest" uses whatever he can get his hands on to take care of himself and provide for his own ease—just as some birds line their nests with feathers and down to make them more comfortable.

2. **Fair-Weather Friends:** This term comes from yachting. Almost any friend will go sailing with you in "fair weather"—but only true friends will help you handle the boat in foul weather.

3. **Fortnight:** The word is just a contraction of "fourteen nights."

4. **Flickers:** In the early days of the motion pictures there was little synchronization between the film and the projector—and so the actors seemed to twitch and jerk and the pictures "flickered" instead of moving forward smoothly as they do today.

270

5. **Good Egg:** There is, perhaps, more difference between "good" and "bad" in eggs than in any other common article. So, to make the differentiation clear, people are called either good or bad "eggs."

6. **Sports Fan:** The sports fan is a spectator so enthusiastic that his actions are rabid; he is a fanatic—hence, a "fan."

7. **Fork Over:** The hand looks something like a pitchfork and to "fork over" or "out" was originally to hand out lavishly—as one would when spreading with a pitchfork.

8. **Edifice, Edify:** Both words are Latin. "Edifice" means "a building" or "house" and "edify" literally means "to build a house." If we instruct in a methodical manner, building from the ground up just as a house is built, we truly "edify."

9. **Foil:** A "stooge" is called a "foil" in allusion to the metal "foil" used by jewelers to set off precious stones.

10. **Like Fun:** Originally this meant "energetically and with great delight." Then we said it sarcastically, with just the opposite meaning—and now the phrase just means "no."

11. **Good Friday:** The term comes from "God's Friday"—since Christ was crucified on that day.

12. **Play Both Ends against the Middle:** This is an old gambling expression used in reference to prize fights, cock fights, and other matches between two contestants. A person who bet on both contestants was said to be "playing both ends"—and since he was not betting against either, he was said to bet "against the middle."

13. **Make the Eagle Scream:** The miser who holds on to his money tightly may squeeze it so hard that even the silver "eagle" will "scream" out in pain.

14. **Twenty:** This word is just a combination of "two" and "ten."

15. **On the Fence:** The person "on the fence" can, as long as he keeps his balance there, still jump into either field.

16. **Fishy:** The presence of a stale fish about the barn is quickly recognized by its odor. Likewise, we say that something that is suspicious smells. So, by analogy, the suspicious proposition is "fishy."

17. **Foot-Loose:** The allusion is to a horse or other animal that has been hobbled but is now "foot-loose"—it can roam wherever it wishes.

18. **Devil-May-Care:** The "devil-may-care" person is one who, in actions if not in words, says: "The devil may care what I do—but I don't."

19. **Digit:** The word "digit" comes from the Latin *digitus*, meaning either "finger" or "toe"—and when we first began to count we used our fingers and then our toes.

20. **All Fagged Out:** "Fagged" is just a shortening of "fatigued."

∾

ANSWERS—QUIZ 4

1. **Grit:** The term comes from the idea that a strong and fighting rooster will be found to have a great deal of "grit" in his craw. It is a synonym for "guts."

2. **Goodbye:** This word is just a shortening of the phrase, "God be with ye."

3. **Tailor's Goose:** The tailor's pressing iron has a handle that looks like a goose's neck. (The plural of the tailor's "goose," incidentally, is "gooses.")

4. **Gab:** The word "gab" comes from "gabble"—as a goose gabbles—and "gabble" comes from the Irish word *gob*, meaning "mouth."

5. **Guerrilla:** This word is just the diminutive of the Spanish word for "war," *guerra*—and means "little war."

6. **Harmonica:** The device provides a method of playing more than one reed in "harmony." The original "harmonica," however, was a device for playing musical

glasses conceived by Benjamin Franklin. It had pieces written for it by both Mozart and Beethoven. When the reed mouth-organ invented by Damien of Vienna in 1829 came along, it was given the name of Franklin's invention.

7. **Make a Hit:** In the game of cricket, as in the game of baseball, you're successful when you "make a hit."

8. **Hydrophobia:** This is a Greek word and literally means "dread of water." It was once thought—though inaccurately—that dogs suffering from this disease were afraid of water.

9. **Holdup:** The term comes from the fact that the robber almost always tells his victim to "hold up" his hands.

10. **Gilding the Lily:** One cannot make more beautiful an object that already represents the ultimate in beauty.

11. **Hump Oneself:** The person who works himself to the utmost must bend himself to the task—making a "hump" of his back.

12. **Gaffer:** "Gaffer" is just a shortening of "grandfather."

13. **Ginger:** "Hot" spices were once believed to heat the blood and a hot-blooded person was believed to be lively. So, a lively person was said to be full of "ginger" or "pepper."

14. **Horse of Another Color:** The allusion is to the horse trade in which one person tried to switch horses in the middle of the dicker.

15. **Moonshine:** In order to avoid the attention of the "revenooer" illegal stills were, more often than not, operated at night—by "moonshine."

16. **Greengrocer:** The "greengrocer" deals in fresh vegetables and fruits and most of these are green.

17. **Dutch Rub:** Since "Dutch" was once generally applied to all unpleasant things and the Dutch were presumed to be the perpetrators of most distressing tricks, the schoolboy

273

torture of rubbing the hair the wrong way was called a "Dutch rub."

18. **Clink:** This name for a prison comes from the sound of the bolt of the cell lock as it's shot home and also from the "clink" made by the prisoners' leg irons as they drag along the floor.

19. **Horsefeathers:** Although a horse does have "horse-feathers" the whole idea seemed so ridiculous to most people that they began using the term as a synonym for "nonsense."

20. **Flea Bite:** Everyone was at one time presumed to carry fleas about with him. So, something that was no more serious than a "flea bite" was of no consequence.

∾

ANSWERS—QUIZ 5

1. **Chicken Feed:** The corn and other food given chickens is usually cracked or ground into bits; small change is likewise part of the whole. A handful of small change is therefore similar to a handful of "chicken feed"—and is so called.

2. **Wheeze:** The person who has laughed so hard over a joke that he has laughed himself out can only wheeze. So, to call a joke a "wheeze" is to say we have gotten all the laughter we can out of it.

3. **Kidnap:** The "nap" of this word is a variant of "nab," meaning "to steal." To "kidnap" is to steal a child—or "kid."

4. **Jaywalker:** The jay is a saucy bird that pays little attention to anything—even the cat which may be waiting to pounce upon it. A "jaywalker" pays as little attention to the dangers of traffic.

274

5. **Haymaker:** The sweep of the blow of the prize fighter is somewhat similar to the sweep used in cutting "hay" with a scythe—and the blow lays the foe flat just as the scythe mows down the hay.

6. **Quit Your Kidding:** To "kid" was originally to act as foolishly as a child; it was only recently that it acquired the additional meaning of "to poke fun."

7. **Off the Track:** This expression comes from hunting. When the dogs lose the scent they are "off the track." The concept of a train going "off the track" was a later addition that added emphasis.

8. **Kick the Bucket:** The man about to hang himself will mount a bucket or other support, tie the rope, and then "kick the bucket" out from under.

9. **Keeled Over:** The expression is nautical. When a ship is turned over by the wind it's "keeled over"—since then the keel is above water.

10. **Icky:** "Icky" is just a shortening of the word "sticky." It sounds more unpleasant, however.

11. **Inning:** The term comes from cricket. The team at bat is "in"; the team on the field is "out"; and so, a time at bat is called an "inning."

12. **Jockey:** The name "John" and its variants are general terms for a man. A steeple jack is a "steeple man"; a jack-in-the-box, a "man-in-the-box"; a "jockey," as indicated by the diminutive, a little man—from the desire in horse racing to reduce the weight carried by the horse.

13. **Kingdom Come:** This synonym for heaven comes from the "Lord's Prayer"—"Thy kingdom come."

14. **G-Man:** The "G" stands for Government—although the term is only applied to investigators of the Department of Justice. Treasury Department investigators are some times called "T-men."

15. **Burn Up the Dust:** If your wagon or chariot or automobile is going fast enough, the friction of its tires upon the earth will create enough heat—at least figuratively—to "burn up the dust."

16. **Blockhead:** The allusion is to the wooden "block" on which a man once kept his wig.

17. **Give Her the Gun:** When a motor, particularly an airplane engine, is turning over at full throttle it sounds like a machine gun—and so, to open the throttle is to "give her the gun."

18. **Heavy:** The old-time theatrical villain was generally a brute. To look and act the part it was necessary for the performer to be "heavy" in body, features, and voice.

19. **Buttonhole:** When we "buttonhole" a person we figuratively—or literally—hold him by a button. The pun on "buttonhold" is probably intended.

20. **Scram:** "Scram" is just short for "scramble"; when we get out of the way as fast as possible, we scramble.

❧

ANSWERS—QUIZ 6

1. **High-Brow:** It was once believed that the bumps on the head indicated one's abilities and sensibilities. A "high brow" was presumed to denote great intellect.

2. **Mother-of-Pearl:** The pearl is a special growth, a sort of tumor, that develops as a part of the inner lining of the pearl shell—hence this lining is called "mother-of-pearl."

3. **Square Shooter:** The allusion is to Freemasonry—as in the phrase "on the square." A "square shooter" would only shoot for good cause.

4. **Lunatic:** The Romans believed that insane people were "moon-struck," and that their insanity increased as the moon waxed full. *Luna* is the Latin word for "moon."

5. **Greased Lightning:** "Lightning" is known to move very fast; when it's "greased" it should go even faster.

6. **Lionize:** The hostess who succeeds in bagging some especially prominent guest generally makes a to-do over him—and her achievement—very much like the hunter who proudly points out the "lion" among his hunting trophies.

7. **Pithy:** The "pith" is at the heart of the stalk; a "pithy" remark goes straight to the heart of the matter.

8. **Gilt-Edged:** The best stocks and bonds were once printed with a "gilt edge"; the promoters of purely speculative concerns didn't bother.

9. **La-Di-Da:** This is just a humorous imitation of the fine speech lavished on ladies of fashion by their attentive beaux—and returned by the ladies.

10. **Chipper:** When a bird is feeling especially good it chirrups and "chippers"—so, too, does a person.

11. **Cameleopard:** This name for a giraffe is just a combination of "camel" and "leopard." The animal's head and neck are like a camel's; its spots are like a leopard's.

12. **Shaver:** A "shaver" is a "chip off the old block"—but a little one, a "shaving."

13. **Automobile:** Two words are combined in this term—the Greek *autos*, meaning "self," and the Latin *mobile*, meaning "moving." An automobile is "self-moving."

14. **Spindling:** The allusion here is to the "spindle" of the spinning wheel—which is both long and thin.

15. **Milksop:** A "milksop" is literally a piece of bread sopped in milk; it's formless, without any strength or solidity.

16. **Backwater Village:** As the age of commerce developed, those communities which were located on the coast and the main waterways grew and prospered, while those on lesser streams and "backwater" inlets remained small and unimportant.

17. **Don't Care a Hang:** This expression, used to indicate complete indifference to consequences, is but a shortening of "I don't care if I hang for it."
18. **Downright:** "Downright" is just another way of saying "right down"—and the reference is to being "right down to earth."
19. **Lingo:** "Lingo" is good Latin somewhat corrupted; the Latin word for "language" is *lingua*.
20. **Moon-Struck:** A person in love is likely to act just as crazily as a lunatic—and the ancient Romans believed the "moon" made men mad.

∾

ANSWERS—QUIZ 7

1. **Playing Possum:** When an opossum is cornered, it feigns death—so, too, does the person "playing possum."
2. **Nose for News:** We say we "smell out" things that are hidden—in allusion to a terrier locating a rat—and we call a person who "smells out" such things "nosey." And so, a person who smells out news items has a "nose for news."
3. **Potboiler:** In olden times a pot was kept simmering on the fire all day long and from this pot everyone in the household was fed. In order to eat it was necessary to "keep the pot boiling." So, a book written primarily to get money adds another log to the fire under the pot—and is called a "potboiler."
4. **Egg Money:** The farmer's wife generally takes care of the hens. Therefore, the money she gets for selling their eggs is usually considered hers to do with as she wishes—without accounting to her husband for it at all.
5. **On the Dot:** The allusion is to the actual "dot"—found on almost all timepieces—which marks the exact hour or minute.

6. **Ninny:** This is just a diminutive form of "innocent"—though it means a "simpleton" or "fool."

7. **Pug:** "Pug" is short for "pugnacious"—and this word is derived from the Latin *pugnare*, meaning "to fight."

8. **Put That in Your Pipe and Smoke It:** The allusion is to the pipe smoked by American Indians as they sit around their council fires. To put something in your pipe and smoke it is, therefore, to give it consideration.

9. **Dressed Fit to Kill:** The person who is "dressed fit to kill" is out "to make a killing"—"to knock 'em dead."

10. **Penknife:** Men first began to carry small knives in their pockets to sharpen the points of their goose-quill pens—and so pocketknives were called "penknives."

11. **Snowball:** An actual snowball rolling downhill will increase in size rapidly and without effort. Thus anything that multiplies rapidly and with ease is said "to snowball."

12. **Peck Horn:** The alto horn makes a "putt-putt" sound when blown, and the performer on this horn often brings his head forward sharply—just as a chicken does when "pecking" grain.

13. **Party:** When we call a person a "party" we are just using the French term for "person," *partie*—though we usually don't know it.

14. **Get It in the Neck:** The origin of this expression and its meaning are explained by a similar phrase—"where the chicken got the ax." This, too, is the origin of the expression, "sticking your neck out."

15. **Nutty:** A "nutty" person is "off his nut." "Nut" means the head—from its similarity in shape and position to the "nut" on a bolt.

16. **Pandemonium:** The word comes from the Greek *pandaimon* meaning "all the demons."

17. **Picnic:** The "nic" of "picnic" comes from the "knick" of "knicknack"—which means "a trifle." You get your "pick" of "trifles' at a "picnic."
18. **Catty Woman:** You can never tell when a "cat" will turn and scratch you; the same is true of a malicious gossip.
19. **Den:** A man's own room is a sanctuary to which he can retire to lick his wounds—just as a wounded lion returns to its "den."
20. **Gin:** The "gin" of "cotton gin" is just a shortening of the word "engine."

~~

ANSWERS—QUIZ 8

1. **Prune, Lemon:** An unpleasant person has a "sour" disposition—hence, is a "lemon." A sour taste makes one pucker up the face into many wrinkles—whence, "prune."
2. **Corned Beef:** Any small grain was at one time called a "corn"—even a grain of salt. Thus salted beef came to be called "corned beef."
3. **On the Q.T.:** So quiet that you can't even mention the word, and can merely indicate it by the first and last letters: "Q" and "T."
4. **Shinny:** The boy who "shinnies" up a tree actually uses his shins in the operation.
5. **Scalp Lock:** Many Indian tribes shaved their heads until there was just a single lock of hair left on the scalp. This, however, was sufficient for an enemy to use in removing the scalp—and it was left there as a challenge.
6. **Worth His Salt:** Since the Latin *salarium* means "salt money," a man "worth his salt" is worth his salary.
7. **Strike While the Iron Is Hot:** Cold iron cannot be shaped by a blacksmith.

8. **Slicker:** "Slicker" and "sleek" both come from the same root—the Middle English *slike*, meaning "to polish" or "make smooth." The slicker is sleek—a "smoothy."

9. **Stumping:** When a politician "stumps" the country, he goes from town to town—and in each makes a speech appealing for votes by climbing up on a stump.

10. **Siesta:** This noonday nap got its name from the Spanish *seis*, meaning "six." Noon is the old "sixth hour" of the day.

11. **Shower:** At this type of party given a bride-to-be, gifts are "rained" down upon her.

12. **Red-Handed:** The allusion is to the hand of the murderer, coated with blood.

13. **Wife:** The word is from the Anglo-Saxon *wif*. *Wefan* means "to weave" and in the form *wif* refers to the wife's duty of weaving the family clothes.

14. **Slipshod:** "Slipshod" literally means "wearing slippers"; the person who wears slippers and scuffs about is careless in dress and can generally be presumed to be careless in work.

15. **Outlandish:** The ways and speech of the foreign person often seem to us odd and unusual—and "outlandish" literally means "foreign."

16. **Spike His Guns:** In the days when cannon were fired by putting a brand to the touchhole it was possible to put them out of commission by driving an iron "spike" into this hole.

17. **Poles Apart:** The "poles" referred to are the North and South Poles. No two spots on this earth are farther apart.

18. **Savvy:** This synonym for "knowledge" comes from the Spanish phrase *save usted*, meaning "do you know?"—influenced by the French verb *savoir*.

19. **Sissy:** This term is a diminutive of "sis," and "sis" is a contraction of "sister."

20. **Groundwork:** The allusion is to the erection of a building. The very first thing that has to be done is the excavation —the "groundwork."

∼

ANSWERS—QUIZ 9

1. **Fit to a T:** The allusion is to the "T-square" used by architects and draftsmen—and so means "exactly as on the drafting board."
2. **Tar:** Sailors are called "tars" from the tar they once used in caulking their ships, the tar they once put on their pigtails, and the tarpaulins they once wore.
3. **Put One's Shoulder to the Wheel:** In early stagecoach days the passengers were all supposed to turn out when the coach got stuck in the mud and "put their shoulders to the wheel" to get it free.
4. **Fish Story:** No type of story is so often exaggerated as the angler's story of "the big one that got away."
5. **Guinea Hen:** This type of fowl was believed to have been brought to Europe from Guinea, Africa. Actually, however, it probably came from India.
6. **Brewing Storm:** A storm is said to "brew" because the clouds that foretell its approach appear similar, in the way they pile up, to a batch of beer mash that is "brewing."
7. **Under One's Wing:** The allusion is to a hen that takes her own baby chicks—and, at times, a few strays—"under her wing" for protection when danger threatens.
8. **Kick Over the Traces:** If a harnessed horse gets excited enough, it will literally kick its legs "over the traces."
9. **Under a Cloud:** The grace of kings was once compared to the light of the sun. Those who were out-of-favor did not receive this sunlight—and so, perforce, were "under a cloud."

10. **Togs:** The ancient Roman wore a circular piece of cloth wrapped around his shoulders which he called a *toga*. From this comes our word "togs."

11. **Resting On One's Oars:** This is a nautical expression and is generally used in reference to a longboat manned by several hands. The man who "rests on his oars" stops rowing—and so is not "pulling his weight" in the boat.

12. **Yum-Yum:** When you sigh with satisfaction and lick your lips, both at the same time, the sound produced is very similar to "yum-yum."

13. **Umbrella:** "Umbrella" is a Latin word; it means "little shadow."

14. **Tread the Boards:** At one time the actors' stage was made of boards placed on trestles—and so the actors literally "trod the boards."

15. **Ax to Grind:** Sometimes one farmer drops in on another just to pass the time of day; but more often than not it later develops that he has brought along an ax he'd like to grind on his neighbor's grindstone.

16. **Give a Man Enough Rope:** There is a double allusion in this expression—to an animal's tether and the hangman's rope. If you tether a horse on a long enough rope, he will ultimately entangle himself in it. If you give a man enough "rope," or leeway, he will ultimately entangle himself in his own lies—and, figuratively, slip the hangman's noose around his own neck.

17. **Have His Wings Clipped:** A cock, hen, or other domestic fowl that "flies too high" will have its wings clipped—so it can never "fly the coop."

18. **Put Up or Shut Up:** This phrase is small-boy talk and means—"Put up your fists and fight or stop talking big."

19. **Wow:** If a theatrical performance is good the audience will applaud and cheer; if it's extremely good—an outstanding success—they may even shout "Wow!"

20. **Bigwig:** At one time all men of importance in England wore wigs—lawyers and judges still do—and, it was then presumed, the bigger the wig, the more important the man.

∽

ANSWERS—QUIZ 10

1. **Pearl Diver:** Like the true pearl diver, the dishwasher dives down into the water and comes up with something white. It might be an oyster, but—unfortunately—it's just another dish.

2. **Undertaker:** People have long disliked the task of burying the dead—even the terms associated with it. For this reason, the man who was once called a "gravedigger" is now called an "undertaker"—since he "undertakes" this unpleasant task. Undertakers themselves now prefer to be called "morticians."

3. **Gangway:** The passages between bulkheads aboard ship are called "gangways"—from the Anglo-Saxon *gangweg*, "a way for going"—and these passages are often long and narrow. A sailor carrying a coil of rope or any other object along one of these passages would call, "Out of the gangway" to those who blocked his way. This was quickly shortened to just "Gangway!"

4. **Soup and Fish:** Since American meals are generally rather simple, with only one or two courses, it's only at an affair calling for formal dress that a man is likely to be served both soup and fish before the main course. So, formal dress and "soup and fish" quite naturally go together.

5. **Earmark:** We say a thing permanently set aside for a definite use has been "earmarked" because English farmers used to notch the ears of their cattle to permanently identify them. Hog's ears are "earmarked" to this day.

284

6. **Coffin Nail:** Lecturers against the evils of smoking gave us this name for a cigarette. They proclaimed that each cigarette smoked was "another nail in your coffin"—and often went to the trouble of having a real coffin on-stage with them to emphasize their point.

7. **Lead a Dog's Life:** In the Orient the dog is thoroughly despised; he's considered the scavenger of the streets and must look to the gutters for such scraps of food as he can pick up. Anyone who lives such a life must be very miserable indeed.

8. **Spider:** Frying pans once had long legs like spiders; they were placed right over the coals on the hearth and stood up on their own legs.

9. **Phiz:** "Phiz" comes from "physiognomy" and "physiognomy" refers to the contours of the face.

10. **Indian File:** Indians used to walk in single file through the forests—following in each other's footsteps. The last Indian would obliterate the footprints of his companions so that they could not be tracked down by pursuers.

11. **Middy Blouse:** The loose blouse with a sailor collar that girls wear is called a "middy blouse" because it looks just like the blouse worn by the "middy" or midshipman aboard a battleship.

12. **Past Master:** This term comes from Freemasonry. A "past master" is one who has previously been the head of a lodge. Since the master must obviously know all there is to know about the order, a "past master" can logically be presumed to know even more.

13. **One Swallow Does Not Make a Summer:** In ancient Greece the swallow was supposed to herald the approach of summer. Indeed, the children were given a holiday from school when the first swallow appeared. But if you see just a single swallow, you can't be sure it's summer

yet. Similarly, in life, you can't hope for too much from just a single sign.

14. **Show His True Colors:** The allusion here is to the privateer or pirate whose ship flew the flag of a friendly nation when approaching a prize. It "travelled under false colors" until it was within cannon shot. Then the pirate or privateer lowered the flag he was flying and raised his true flag —and so "showed his true colors."

15. **Cent:** The Latin *centum* means "one hundred"; there are one hundred "cents" in the dollar.

16. **A Run for Your Money:** The expression comes from horse racing. If the horse you've placed your bets on does not win but still makes a fairly good showing, it at least gives you "a run for your money."

17. **Bee:** Honeybees all work, and all work together, for the good of the hive. Human beings who get together on a similar cooperative work project call it a "bee."

18. **Buck:** The dandy who tosses his head and shows his strength in front of the ladies is just like the male deer, or "buck," that tosses its antlers and shows its strength before the does.

19. **Varsity:** "Varsity" is just a shortened form of "university."

20. **Zwieback:** This form of bread is baked twice—and that is what its name literally means. The German *zwei* means "two" and *backen* means "to bake."